Contents

Foreword

This is a beautiful collection of everything we feel and don't feel – what we say and can't say. It is a delicately woven tapestry of human life, collected by a stranger who offered an ear to listen without judgement and who has the depth of soul to interpret the complicated layers of love.

I have walked with Matt, enjoyed his company hugely and found myself wanting to tell him the secrets of my heart. He has an uncanny and admirable ability to make people want to divulge truths they may never have revealed to anyone and, in sharing them so discreetly in this book, he allows us all to learn more about the thing that makes each of our lives unique – our experience and understanding of love.

Clare Balding

The Journey

Five Hundred Miles on Foot through Scotland

I'm not too sure where the idea of journeying by foot through Scotland emerged from. It continued on from a previous journey I had made, from Avebury in Wiltshire to Lindisfarne on the Northumberland coast, which had connected sacred places in the landscape of Britain, so it seemed natural to set off for Scotland from Lindisfarne and head for Callanish on the Isle of Lewis as a route through the land from the North Sea to the Atlantic. I wanted to cross a frontier, to experience the cultural shift from one perceived nation to another. I wanted to tell the stories of folk from both sides of that imagined border and see how the stories morphed and changed as I made my way westwards and then north. I wanted to experience Scotland while decisions about sovereignty, ownership and belonging were being explored.

Along the way I sought hospitality, a bed for the night, food, shelter, a welcome. I moved as a stranger through the land looking for connection, searching out the narratives that shape this part of the world. As ever, I sought to connect with people through the stories of their heart – those stories of love that have formed their human experience profoundly. I met with folk on the path, in the pub, by the shore, in the city and in the villages. We spent time listening to each other's stories, opening up a little, shedding some tears, testing our vulnerabilities, exploring our truths.

I found Scotland to be the place I had longed for it to be – a place of passion and colour, of people and landscapes that cascade the senses and move the spirit. Earth, sky and sea shaped my movements through the land, and Scotland stays in my memory now as a place of sacred union, where the hard lines dissolve a little and the beauty and spirit of the earth finds an essential space.

Here is a collection of the human love stories, heard and shared on this 500-mile journey through Scotland in the months of March and April. They are not perfect: but they are perfect. They do not resolve, begin or end as fictional stories might. They start where we found ourselves meeting on that day – with those experiences we were going through at the time. They meander and sometimes end abruptly. Each story reflects an experience of love and connection. They explore our desires to be heard and seen and touched and wanted – our desire to belong. They express the importance of 'home', of 'welcome' and 'connection'. They are sad, joyful, ecstatic, hard, glorious, life-long and momentary. They are all of our stories for they explore the human heart, our human condition. And, though I walked through Scotland, the essence of these stories could have been heard anywhere around the world because, in the end, we are all lovers and hermits, brothers and sisters, sons and daughters, migrants and refugees. We are all lost and all found.

Listening

To hear someone deeply is one of the greatest gifts you can offer a person. It is the essential act of love. In that exchange, you allow a person to be recognised, to be noticed, to be seen. It is an act of profound compassion. It is a love story in itself.

As I walked five hundred miles through Scotland, I sought to provide spaces where people could be deeply heard. In these spaces, people were allowed to be vulnerable, to open out and share anything and everything. Together we nurtured a heart space, a place for loving interaction and compassionate understanding.

Through sharing stories of love and connection, people give something of themselves to their listener, allowing themselves to be 'seen', to be understood, to be acknowledged. In this listening space, people have the opportunity to heal, to learn, to grow.

In allowing these stories to be recorded, to be written and shared around the world, the people who feature in this book are extending that conversation, that loving dialogue. This book provides a space where understanding across nations and cultures can grow. Fear can subside, the 'stranger' can become more familiar. Our human experience becomes a shared endeavour. We are no longer alone because we can be understood and can understand others.

In its most pure form, I believe that hearing another person deeply and compassionately is a sacred act. The essential loving act, it is love made and given.

'It doesn't matter what path you walk,
what matters is the heart you walk it in'

Alastair McIntosh

•

'Human beings need stories'

Paul Auster

1. It Wasn't a Fleeting Thing

The journey begins, through the sea and the mud, as the tide ebbs and the land emerges from the wash. After walking some time I come to a standstill by the water's edge in Berwick-upon-Tweed. Further on, a day from here, perhaps, I will cross that invisible line into a different land, into Scotland. The path stretches out before me. The light loosens its grip. The harbour moves restlessly.

·

We met when I went to work in a kibbutz in Israel. I'd been working in London, working as a waitress in a café, and I was waiting to go to university in London. And I didn't have anything to do for the summer and I thought I'd go to a kibbutz. I didn't even know where Israel was and I didn't know what a kibbutz was, but it was somewhere for me to go because I had no one to go on holiday with. I thought, 'That sounds nice – it'll be warm, something to do.' I arrived in Tel Aviv airport – I didn't know what I was doing. I spoke to a guy at the airport who looked like he knew what he was doing and he told me what buses to take. It was all quite random, really. I had to take a bus and get off at a junction and then walk and wait for a lift. And it was back in the early eighties, when many young people, and also the soldiers, travelled around by hitching. So that's what I did. Eventually this guy rolled by. I was just standing there with my thumb out and he was going to the kibbutz, so he took me along.

So I arrived at this kibbutz. I got to speak to the volunteer leader and he said, 'You can stay in the volunteer houses and we'll speak to you tomorrow morning.' There was a kind of club place that people would go to and meet, so that evening I went with some of the other volunteers up to this club and I met Uzi. He and his friend were sitting outside. His friend said, 'Hello, who are you?' It was a small community and I was a different face, I guess. We spoke for a while, but I'd got up early that day so I didn't stay long. The following evening there was a disco. There was always a disco in the same club – and it was a pyjama party! So I had these pyjamas on – fabulous old men's striped pyjamas – and I got to the party and I saw Uzi again. I was kind of dancing with different people and then I saw him leave and I didn't know if he'd noticed that I was there – we didn't speak! So I went and sat on the wall outside and Uzi came by. And he looked like he was leaving. He said, 'Hello, how are you doing? What are you doing here? I have to go and water the cotton fields. Do you want to come with me?' And I just thought, 'Yeah.' So the next minute we're driving out into the fields, driving through sweetcorn – I'd never seen sweetcorn. Driving out and then parking up and looking out at the view. And Uzi was showing me that the closest place to us was actually an Arab village and that they lived very peacefully together with the kibbutz. And I just was really touched by that. It was abroad, it was warm. We had the music and the stars.

Great music. Just the whole scene was like bliss with this lovely guy, with these beautiful eyes.

Wow!

And I had this pyjama top on and this pair of shorts, and I was thinking, 'I can't believe it.' I've just been waitressing, doing these mad shifts up until two days ago, and here I am in the middle of this field. You know, I hadn't known what to expect but I hadn't expected anything like that.

I felt a kind of 'at home-ness' with him. And I remember Uzi putting his head on my legs. There was a kind of, I want to use the word comfort, if you know what I mean, in a kind of 'home' way. I thought, 'This is a really nice feeling.' Rather than being overcome by some passion – it was bigger, it was more than that. It wasn't a fleeting kind of thing. This was a kind of 'Oh, I feel totally fine with this.'

But I was only there for that weekend. I wasn't allowed to stay in the kibbutz. So when I left on Sunday morning he gave me the keys to his flat and the address and he said, 'If you don't find anything, you can stay in this flat.' But I got into Tel Aviv and I sorted out another place, so I took his key back to the kibbutz organisation and I went to a kibbutz up north near Acre. A couple of weekends later there was a phone call one night – it was Uzi. He said, 'There's a beach trip planned and I wondered if you wanted to come along and join us.' So I went and spent a bit of time with him before I travelled down to the south of Israel.

What I remember is that Uzi gave me this photo of himself. I couldn't believe that someone that handsome thought I was attractive. Honestly. I really didn't. I just used to think I could never find a photo of myself as nice as that. Oh, I think I was completely lovelorn. Do you know that expression? I don't think I could concentrate on anything. I returned to the UK and started my first year at university in London. I went to university as a mature student and I worked. But really I couldn't think. My heart wasn't in it because all I could think about was him.

And the next summer I went back as a guest and I stayed with Uzi for that summer. Worked on the kibbutz and I was Uzi's guest? girlfriend? I spent a few months there and then I came back to Britain – I think I had a re-sit or something. But I decided I would just go back to live in Israel with him. So I just left London. I came home first to Scotland. My parents were living in Gullane. I thought, 'That's it, I'm going back!' And I had this friend who said, 'Mand, if you love him, then you've got to go after him.'

And we have been together ever since.

Yeah. It's a bit about knowing somebody. Accepting. It's about giving space to someone and it's also about what you share. And still being interested. You know.

And do you know something? If I had to capture an image it would be this – I'm sitting in the dining room and it's late lunchtime and then I see Uzi coming in. And he comes in and he's got these woollen socks and his work boots on and he's kind of tripping into the dining room. And he's picking up his tray and he's looking round the dining room and then he sees me. And he does this kind of double blink.

He does this double blink, with this beautiful smile, and he sees me. He sees me. I would capture that, just that.

2. How I Met Harry

Each weary footstep carries me further – along miles of coastline, scoured beaches and cliff-top promontories. England gives way to Scotland. I cross that cultural, political and national divide – the sun shines the same on either side, the marram grass gently beckons me onwards, into the strong air.

•

This story of how I met Harry is so ridiculous. I was volunteering with Greenpeace. I was working on a ship with them and we had made port in Stornoway, in the Outer Hebrides. Long story short, we had to do this flight over to Ireland to find fishing trawlers to do an action on. So we chartered this plane to Ireland. They said, 'Lily, we're going to send you to use the equipment and figure it out, and you're going to have to go to Ireland for five days and just wait there until the ship comes and makes port in Galway and we come pick you up.' They said, 'Here's some money, find a hostel there, whatever, there you go!' I was like eighteen at the time and thought, 'This is really cool.'

And so we fly over to Ireland. We land and this pilot says, 'Where am I bringing you?' And I said, 'The closest hotel or whatever works.' He said, 'Oh well, I live on this farm with my family, and I have a son that's your age and a daughter that's a year older and another daughter that's younger, and you should come stay with us if you want.'

So I just show up on this farm in Ireland with like beautiful, green, verdant fields. And they raise cows – it's this organic cow farm! Jerry, who's the father, is a pilot and his son, Harry, is also a pilot, so when they're back here they have this hangar with these teeny little planes. And they were like, 'Oh, do you wanna go up for a spin in the plane?' They're just the most genuine people. I don't even know how to describe it – just the most real people, just kind, unapologetic. They just welcomed me in. I was this Greenpeace person. I was all pierced and vegetarian and eighteen and I was like 'I know everything about the world!' but, actually, in reality, I know nothing! But they just said, 'Come.' They wouldn't take my money, they wouldn't take anything, and it was just like this respite, having been on a ship for about two and a half months at this point, having this family to be part of.

I left but we remained in touch. They said, 'Cool, whenever you wanna come back, then please do.' And it turns out that I've gone back almost every year for Christmas. They're like a second family to me now. That family unit is so unlike what my family unit was like because my parents are no longer together, so we never really had that space that we all had together and were present for each other. So to be welcomed into that was such a blessing. Yeah, I have a lot of love for them. I think there's definitely sadness that comes from needing to work through some of what my own family situation was like. But then that beauty as well, I guess, from being so welcomed. Sometimes it's crazy how they can be so close together – that feeling of sadness but also of joy.

It's almost surreal because the story itself is sort of like serendipity. And it's almost hard to accept sometimes – if you are used to this conditionality of love, this expectation of something else that isn't just that pure 'release', that giving without anything in return. I'm kind of like, 'Woh, I don't know what to do with this.' And then to have maintained that relationship and still have that connection and resonance, and then the growth everyone in that family has gone through that you've been able to witness, and them of me too. Yeah, it's just been this huge teacher in my life, a really wonderful example of love.

I've definitely always said that they're my second family, but I think really delving into what that means shows the dimensionality of love. It by no means illegitimises the love that you have with your own family, it just shows you that there is this spectrum, this depth and width to it that's so nuanced and so complex but basic as well.

3. Shrapnel and Flowers

Just above the beach, facing out to sea, stands a row of park benches that frame the elegant grass lawns. Here, walkers walk dogs and folk huddle together, like cardboard cut-outs swaying stiffly in the sea breeze. I pause to take in the scene and am confronted by an energetic women armed with a ball, a retrieving dog, a wonderful sense of humour, and a gregariously told love story.

•

When we were young, my mother and father were original Independent Labour Party people, you know. We went to an organisation called the Socialist Sunday School. We lived in Glasgow, and during the war my father was a Rolls-Royce engineer who built Spitfires. As a result of the working conditions during the war he took TB and he died when we were all quite young. Anyway, that's by the by! In the Socialist Sunday School we learned the basics of what socialism meant, and that was where we also learned our love of the outdoors – we went camping, rambling and we went hostelling. We met every Sunday all through the year and then, on May Day, we had a big celebration. But when we got to become teenagers, we were looking for a little more than this. The Labour Party had a youth movement called the Young Socialists. They got a bit too left-wing so they got disbanded. So what did we all do, young budding socialists? We all joined the Young Communist League. It was 1955. I was seventeen. I lived in Glasgow, I was a Young Communist and I sang in the Young Communist Choir. And we went to Warsaw to a World Youth Peace Festival – and Warsaw was interesting because when you walked through the town every building either had shrapnel or flowers in it because it was just ten years after the war.

And there was an obvious generation, particularly the men, who were just not there. The Poles suffered horrendously in the war. At the festival, I was one of the Scottish dancers in this group. We arrived there and we met a group of Polish folk dancers and I fell madly in love with one of them. He was called Leszek – Leszek Kalinowski – who I've now found out is some sort of professor in Krakow or somewhere. I'm pleased to say he has stayed and not left Poland because there's a lot to be said for the old system! We stayed in touch for a while but it wasn't really practical, so it fizzled out. I've been married twice since then. I've lived all over the world, and wherever I've been I've got involved with teaching kids to dance. I had this international school group in Dar es Salaam and I had another group of these silly boys in Sri Lanka. Wherever I've been, I've always done dancing, and it's just lovely, you know. And all these kids get a wee bit of Scotland in them, wherever they go. It's good. It's good, you know. For me, love is socialism, it's common ownership and control. I'll start quoting the precepts, you know: 'It's common ownership and control of these things we need in order to live happily and well.'

4. Love Is Just Being

Each part of me aches now. Each step seems to jar my body. I shudder along the road, tripping past villages, bumbling through golf courses. I long to be still, I yearn for silence. I miss the sea – that wide expanse of sky and ether. I am only sixty miles into a 500-mile journey west and then north. I am a stranger here, a foreigner seeking connection. I am a revolving door of arrivals and departures, a brief encounter on the path.

·

At that time I felt so far away from my home. I felt so far away from everybody that, I guess, I'd ever been close to. And I think I was trying to reach out to them, hoping that in the time I was away I would be able to somehow resolve it. To rebuild that connection that had been broken. And then it was funny because, in being away, that didn't actually happen – I wasn't able to resolve it at all. It made me really sad and it made me cry because we've been through a lot.

I'd always longed to travel, and I'd got to an age and a stage where I hadn't gone to the places I thought I was going to. I wanted to see new things. I wanted to get outside and be outside with nature and walk mountains and just be elevated and have something that wasn't here, like the UK, or things that I already knew, or even Europe. I wanted to leave the safety-net of Europe because I'd never left before. I left to try and get some equilibrium back, to try and get some balance, and that space was incredible. To be away and have that sense of perspective and look back. And especially 'cause I'd gone to the other side of the planet. You see your life completely differently, and you see the things you do have and you see the people that you love and the things that you're from and the things that make you up and the things that make sense. At the time it didn't make any difference that there were literally countries and oceans between me and the things I'd left. Those bonds are still really strong.

I'd run away and I still loved somebody. But I couldn't make it work. I tried – we tried – and we couldn't seem to work it through. So it was really painful. I completely hadn't expected it at all and I came apart.

I was thinking generally about love and what love is – whether it's with people, places, things. And I realised I think I struggle to talk about it because, for me, sadly, my association with love now, very specifically with other people and my ex, is so much bound up with grief as well. With grief and loss. And that's so painful – I wouldn't know how to begin that dialogue. There's so much loss there that I'm trying to heal from.

I think it was love in its brightest sense – I think?

I don't know because I haven't really loved that much. I've not been in love much. Like I spent a lot of my life loving people or having a fondness of people from afar, and then, when I actually finally fell in love, I really, really fell. I almost fell too deeply, to the point that when I needed to find a way out I couldn't! It's hard because I struggle to remember the brightness and the loveliness of that time – because there's such an association now with a period of being not OK. So it's almost like the journey's kind of gone and I'm somewhere, somewhere beyond that. I don't know where I am on the journey. I feel like a smaller version of myself.

The journey I'm on, I think, is about learning to embrace the good things about yourself. Rather than seeing sensitivity and feeling things strongly as a bad thing, to see it as a good thing, definitely. I think there's a healing in being in the elements and being in nature. And in a way, although it's frightening at times, just being stood on a cliff-top, being buffeted by the wind, to the point that you're being blown off – it's great because it awakens your senses, it makes you feel alive. Yeah, it brings you back to the now.

I just don't think there's enough of a dialogue in society about the things that make me so sad and the things that I'm struggling with – it's the fundamentals of life and there isn't a dialogue there. If there is, I've not found it!

The worst thing about being British is the 'stiff upper lip' culture. I just think people don't know how to really talk. That, to me, is part of the pain that I really struggle with, in terms of a sense of home and finding now where I belong. I think it's being able to find female voices – other women who have gone through the same things and actually being able to talk about it in an open space. And it not be something to be frightened of or something to bury or shove under a carpet.

I think love is just being. I think you can apply that to people, places, your partner, your family. It's just being and sharing and being together and finding a contentedness. It's that stillness. You don't have to try. You're not having to be anything. You're with that person, whoever they are – whether it's a parent, a sibling, a cousin, your partner, the love of your life, like whoever it is – you're accepted.

5. We Don't Like To Say, 'I Love You'

The green makes way to grey, the earth to tarmac, the country blends effortlessly into town. The margins narrow. Figures move faster in straighter lines of purpose, faces down. Amidst the blur and movement of customers, baristas, cake, croissants, dogs, clicking heels, passing heads and laughter, you smile and nod a greeting. We find a corner and you take me to Greece and a beach and a sunset.

•

Two years ago I went to Lesbos, you know, in Greece. I was helping refugees there for some months. And I met a guy there from England. We were waiting on the beach throughout the night, just the two of us, waiting for the boats to come in. Meeting him, I had the most powerful experience that I have ever had in my life, in just two weeks. It was very intense. I had the same feelings in two weeks that I had in my last relationship in one year. It was so powerful. And I think that maybe we fell in love. It was like we connected. I felt like I wanted to be with him for the rest of my life.

After Greece he went to his home and I returned here, and from then we have been meeting each other every two months in different countries. And every time we are together it's like the first time because we are in a different place and travelling and everything is like, 'Wow!'

We don't like to say 'I love you'. We never say it to each other because we think this word is so strong and so important – we don't want to use it if we are not really, really sure. And we think that when people say 'I love you', everything changes. And we use many other words, like 'I miss you'. I know that when I say 'I miss you', it means 'I love you'. Maybe, for me, I know that when I'm in a commitment, something in my brain is saying, 'No, no, no, run away.' It means commitment, and we are afraid of having any long commitment, any serious commitment. When I have a commitment, I feel like it's an obligation – to be with that person because I say I want to be with that person. And I can't change my mind.

I felt very different ten years ago. I had many very long commitments in my life. But I changed my mind and I realised that for me to love, I need to feel free, completely free.

I think the distance is very difficult sometimes because we really miss each other. I think that we have a really strong relationship. Because of the distance we are very sincere with each other, all the time. We always say how we feel. You know, it's very honest, our relationship.

For me, one of the most important things in this relationship is that I can improve myself and I can go wherever I want, by myself, alone. I can take my time if I need it. You know? I don't need him to live my life. For me, that's important. I want to choose to stay with him not because I need to but because I want to – because I'm happier, not because I cannot live without him.

It's mystical, it's magical. I don't know – it's difficult to put into words. I'm still learning – it's difficult to know yourself. I think love is so demanding. You need to know yourself before you love someone, because you cannot love someone if you don't know yourself.

6. You've Been Dumped!

I'm late. I can see you waiting, a figure of uncertain energy, as the cars and traffic move continually past. I feel like I know you, like I've met you many times before, somehow. We flee the noise and the hurry and find a place in the sun, on the earth. The Meadows, warm beneath my legs. You share openly, fiercely and with courage. A local dog seizes his chance, urinating on my boots in the absence of a lead and an owner! He nonchalantly moves away. Stories of belonging and love fall poignantly from you.

·

The project was called 'You've Been Dumped!' and that came about because, on 23rd January 2016, my boyfriend at the time broke up with me. We'd been living together and, actually, I should have seen it coming.

I don't know if it's love exactly because I still haven't understood what that is. But I was very, very attracted to my closest friend at the time, and we'd been friends for almost a year – and I almost slept with him in the August before that. I didn't. I was thinking, 'This isn't happening!' I went back to my boyfriend and said, 'I almost slept with this guy. How do you feel about it?' And he was more or less indifferent – I mean that's the reaction he was giving me. And he sat with a laptop, not really listening, going, 'Whatever, yeah, maybe it would have been OK. I don't know, I can't really tell.' It was very difficult to get any kind of reaction out of him and I thought, 'Oh well, this is shit!' because I actually want some kind of response. It doesn't matter what it is, but in a way it shows that he does care. Though not necessarily! Anyway, I held off from seeing this other guy for a while because I, somehow, still believed in that relationship with my boyfriend. But it was already doomed, so it was only a matter of time. I couldn't avoid what I was feeling for this other person, but I did my best to pretend it didn't exist and that he didn't exist. And then we ended up doing some craft fairs together in the December and we spent more time together and I thought, 'Hmmmm, well, OK!'

I was home alone, actually, on Christmas Day. That was a conscious choice because the only other options were being with my mum, which would have been a complete nightmare for me personally, or going to my boyfriend's family, which would have been even worse! So I chose to be home alone, which was brilliant. I cleaned the boiler cupboard. I had such a good time. I know it sounds terrible but Christmas Day for me was enjoying cleaning the boiler cupboard and not leaving the house for two days. The only person who rang me at Christmas was this friend, actually – the best friend I'd been attracted to. And I was thinking, 'Oh, why are you ringing me, but interesting, thank you, and I really care about you!'

And then he came back sometime during New Year and I

needed help soundproofing my studio. I actually asked twenty different people before I asked him. I didn't want to ask him because I knew I'd have to spend time with him. No one had any time, but he had time. Of course, he had lots of time – he had lots of time to help me soundproof my studio! So we worked on soundproofing my studio almost every day for the first few weeks of January. And something shifted. It was a Monday, and while we were in the same room together I was thinking, 'Oh, there's no way I cannot sleep with this person now.' And I am still officially going out with my boyfriend and we still live together. 'This isn't happening. We've got to have a conversation about this. It's not *not* happening!'

So I went back home with the intention of talking to my boyfriend. He wasn't at home. In fact, he wasn't available to talk at all – Tuesday night, Wednesday night. Thursday night we went to a concert together but it wasn't possible to talk. There was no space. It was an absolute nightmare. What am I supposed to do? I have something to communicate. I don't know what's going to come out of it, but I've got to communicate this thing.

And so on Saturday, after my shift at the market, I got back home. He hadn't slept – he'd been at this all-night party – but I was like, 'God, this is the worst possible moment but, OK, we're going to have a conversation now about how I'm going to sleep with somebody else, and I don't want to but it's going to happen.' Anyway, I shared that with him and he said, 'Right, that's it, I'm moving out.' So he broke up with me and left two hours later.

It was very, very traumatising. There was more to be said until it ended. Maybe it would have ended the next day, but it was like communication had been cut off very suddenly. So that was difficult. I thought, 'I'm not sure how I'm going to deal with this

– I better turn it into a project!' So I trawled the internet for tips on how to survive a relationship break-up. And I found fifty-four tips which I could consider doing, potentially. I didn't do all of them. I systematically worked through as many of them as I could and I think I managed about twenty-two of them. And I rounded up that project on 23rd of January 2017. I decided I'd be test-driving them for a whole year, just to see if I could somehow get over this process of being dumped in the best possible way – like better than every other time up until now. Because I've been dumped a few times but, for whatever reason, I had had a very strong social support network where I was or a job that had given me support. This time I didn't really have that – I was just flailing. I didn't know what to do, so I thought, 'The internet will help!'

There were lots of tips which were easier said than done. And that's why I find it so interesting because they're based on assumptions. Like one of them was 'Reconnect with old friends'. I did. I rang twelve people on one night. Nothing. No one picked up. I mean, seriously, no one rang me back. They didn't even know. Maybe they knew subconsciously that I wanted to talk, but that's not friendship! That's not connection. And it's not as if I'd been estranged from those people – that I hadn't been in touch with them. 'What's going on here? Oh, so if I send you a message on Facebook, you'll respond. Great! But that's not how I roll!' I was so lonely, like awful, awful, terrible. Yeah, and there were other things, like 'Have a girl's night in on the sofa and get drunk and watch a rom-com'. I don't have a sofa, firstly! Secondly, I couldn't find some other women who might be classified as 'girls' to put make-up on with, and I don't have a onesie! I know there are lots of people who have these things but I don't have them and they don't make me feel good!

I bumped into my ex-boyfriend three times on the street, and every single time was at a full moon. And the last time we bumped into each other it was a new moon – so it was obvious that something was shifting, and that was great because a conversation was possible. I had lots of friends with me at the time, so I was thinking, 'OK, I can talk with him.' But it did make me think he could only be a werewolf because these are the only times I am seeing him outside. And while we were living together, he never left his room – like, during daylight hours. And he was a singer-songwriter and he had really melancholic wailing songs, so this got me thinking he must be a werewolf! It's like there's no other possible explanation. I'm more like a daylight person.

I really enjoy researching things – like personal development research is what I'd call it. As in, I like trying to improve my life. The right word there is 'trying' – it doesn't necessarily mean I will! If I detect something that is not going how I would like it to, then I'll identify what it is and do my best to find techniques which other people have used to improve it. And then start trying them out. And it may or may not work. And lots of things do work. It's amazing. And lots of things don't, at all. And I'm thinking, 'Guys, where did you get this from? It doesn't work for me – I can't imagine it works for you either.' And then I turn it into comedy because it's already comical. It's very tragicomic because it is so, so sad. The fact that I feel compelled to do this kind of research is sad – that I even have a need for it. I'd like there to be no need. That it's all just OK. But it's not at all. I thought about this a lot, actually.

In Edinburgh the whole system here is against me – not

personally but against the way I want to live, which is with lots of people in an affordable space, sharing things. In Germany and Austria it was possible to live like that. I lived with ten people, sixteen people, six people. Great, because there's this community there! And it doesn't mean that I'm getting on with all of them at the same time, but if there's some kind of sense of 'home' there, then the support's already there. And then a project like this would probably never happen. I'm not sure if it's going to be possible here. I did my best to create that – I've been here for five years now. Lots of people seem very, very connected on social media – which I am, to some extent, but I don't want to use it for that purpose. I want to meet people in real life; that's what I enjoy. And it's very, very difficult to find that here for me, personally. It was much easier for me abroad because I was a foreigner, so I didn't have to adhere to those social rules – I could just go up to someone. Whereas here, I'm really mindful I've got an English accent and approaching someone might make them say, 'What do you want?'

Actually, I just want to talk!

7. It's the First Forever Thing

In the park, the rain falls steadily. Everything is subdued beneath an enveloping sky. Walkers and dogs keep themselves to themselves. We pass each other by, hands deep in pockets. We pause beneath the dripping canopy, resting on a fallen tree trunk, decaying back to the earth. We talk, share.

.

A part of me still doesn't want to be a father and doesn't want to have a child and doesn't want to be in Scotland. A part of me wants to be wherever I was heading when I set off with a one-way ticket to Asia in 2015. A big part of me wants to still be out there, doing whatever it was that I never knew I was going to do. And as I travelled – and I travelled for six months – I'd travelled with the knowledge that I was going to be a dad. So I had five days in Singapore, where I was travelling, and the rest of the time I carried this – for a time a secret and then a weight and then huge confusion.

And I brought that confusion back and I tried to fit that

around a framework of parenting that I had known, which was a mum and dad who had been together all their lives and raised four kids. I was with a woman whom I wasn't in a relationship with – and with a child you kind of have an expectation to love before you even meet them, when they've kind of fucked your trip. It's very hard.

Since her arrival I have had to negotiate a present and also a future with someone who, in a sense, I don't want in my life – two people I don't want in my life, actually. But while that is the case, there is also the other side of the coin, because they're both amazing resources. They're an amazing opportunity for me to confront myself, an amazing opportunity to create a relationship with someone else. Even if it's not based on romantic love, it's based on a type of love, and a shared love, definitely. A shared love for this other person I am absolutely in love with – my child, Peggy, who is starting to teach me about love in a way that I never knew and a way I've always needed to learn about. But I've been too distracted, too busy to really understand something so permanent, something so forever. But it's also a weight that it's forever – there's a forever-ness about this that I have never, ever experienced. It's the first forever thing.

Guilt is sort of shifting. There's an acceptance there, but it doesn't necessarily make everything OK. I got back from travelling and, on an emotional level, I went into depression, and since then I've gone into anxiety. And of course it's fine not to want to be something, and of course it's fine to not know how to do something – it's natural. I really believe that.

I'm just trying to be honest with myself, but what I haven't been able to do is be honest with others. I've not been able to stand up and say, 'I'm not her husband' or 'I'm not her boyfriend' and 'I'm not in love with her' and 'I'm not able to commit to this' and 'I'm not able to cope with this'. To say that out loud is something that is very, very difficult.

What I don't have is control. What I don't have is the feeling of control. I feel totally like the wheel is out of my hands. I had a panic attack last night like I've never had before. And I was lying on the floor of my kitchen and I couldn't breathe very well, and I had this fundamental feeling that I needed to get out. And I'm still quite rattled from it, partly because I don't know where that came from and I don't know how many more of them I'm going to go through, but partly I'm aware, I'm aware why – it's because I don't have any control and I can't escape, and I want to run away. That's what's happening within, and what's happening without is that I'm having all this lovely time with my daughter. I'm with her and I see her and I'm amazed by her all the time, and I'm in love with her all the time.

And what's so fundamentally exhausting is having to hold both of those things simultaneously, all the time. It's exhausting.

To be so wrecked and incapable and helpless and jarred and anxious and to be so in love.

8. She Was Checking Out My Ass

A breakfast of never-ending pancakes. Outside, the city nonchalantly stirs from its womb-like slumber. A flurry of maps and conversation across the kitchen table. Laughter, confidence and some shyness too. I feel so grateful for your open hearts, for allowing this time of sharing to drift. I can see you in that van now, somewhere across the US, burning brightly, laughing hard!

·

BR: We met at a farm-stand, along the highway, in New Jersey. We both worked at the same place.

DI: We worked at the farm-stand after school. We were sixteen.

BR: And she was checking out my ass as I was sorting apples.

DI: I was . . .

BR: At least that's what she tells me – it was probably plumber's crack!

DI: It was my last day of work and he got up the nerve to ask me out on a date. If you can imagine – he was so shy and quiet. It's, like, totally different from now. I can't even imagine that you were really like that but you were.

BR: We double-dated with the guy who owned the farm-stand and another woman. We went to a place called Gasho's, which was a Japanese restaurant.

DI: We were sixteen – that was fancy!

BR: First date and then what happened? What was the next thing after that?

DI: You arriving in your Boy Scout uniform at my house!

BR: Yeah, yeah, I wanted to earn some points. So I was in the Boy Scouts – that's the kind of guy I was.

DI: He was an Eagle Scout, by the way. Very impressive! I don't know if you know about that?

BR: I showed up at her house in my Boy Scout uniform.

DI: You just happened to come by when my parents were there!

BR: Her dad – well, that kind of stuff means a lot to him. You know, he's always been that type of person. Not that I really knew it at the time, but I figured, 'How can you go wrong?'

DI: We were sixteen when we met and I was twenty-three when we got married. Now we're fifty-five. High school sweethearts!

BR: So we started dating, and in her senior year she ends up going on exchange, leaving the country to go to Holland for a year. So we had this long-distance thing where I ran up some huge phone bills with my parents. They were never happy about it!

DI: So at sixteen he proposed to me because he was terrified I was going to meet some Dutch guy in Holland!

BR: And then, when she got off the plane, she wouldn't kiss

me. After a year! I couldn't believe it. I was heartbroken. Explain yourself!

DI: Well, you know, I was so young and it was a whole year that I hadn't seen you. I just wasn't quite sure. I had to get to know you again, you know. A year's a long time! He never forgives me for that.

BR: My heart exploded!

DI: And then we went to university. I was in New York City going to university and he was in Maine. So for four years we had a long-distance relationship.

BR: It was nine hours' driving from Diana, and no one flew then. We saw each other on vacations, holidays, summer, maybe. I worked for her parents – they had a hotel in northern New York. We used to send these love letters to each other.

DI: Yeah, I saved them. I still have them.

BR: I used to record our favourite songs on cassette and send her the cassette. You know, that kind of thing. And she'd send me one back and I'd drink a beer and I'd cry.

It's so funny – the kids found the letters one time and they were reading them.

DI: Did they?

BR: Yes. And I remember her laughing so hard. You have a picture of your parents in your mind, right? And then you read this other version of their life and you think, 'That doesn't make sense!' There was one point in college – the third year – that was a little rocky, and Diana split up with me.

DI: Yeah, I did.

BR: She had to go and sow some wild oats and figure out if I was the one!

DI: I broke up with him because he was getting so serious. He wanted to get married. I wasn't ready for it.

BR: I was ready.

DI: He was ready, and I was scared and wondering, 'What the heck? Which road am I taking here? Am I gonna get married and settle down or am I going to be this independent woman and go off and do other things?' But what did it last? Like two weeks?

BR: A month, I think. It felt like six, but it was a month.

DI: I remember sitting in my apartment and you calling me on the phone. And we weren't supposed to be talking because I had broken up with you! And he called me, like nothing happened. 'Hey, do you wanna go dancing tonight?' he says. I'll never forget that phone call. And I gave in, like, 'Yeah, that sounds good.' And that was it!

So, at the end of university, when he finished and I finished, we decided to join the Peace Corps. We joined the Peace Corps and then realised that we couldn't go together unless we were married. So that was kind of a push, and we thought, 'OK, so let's get married.'

The fun thing now, at this age, is to try and have an exciting life together and to see the world and do different things, but together.

BR: It's one of those journeys, and you get to a certain point and it just kind of went!

DI: Yeah, time goes by.

BR: And you ask these questions that make you think back. So Diana is fifty-five, I'm fifty-five. We started dating at sixteen, so it's been almost forty years that we've known each other. I know, it doesn't seem like it. Because I still don't feel like fifty-five. But it has been a good journey. And they all have their ups and downs, and there's always things that happen that – how shall I say it? – that cast new light on things.

We've always been together – we've never really been apart, other than that time in college, right? Our kids think we argue about things and they give us a hard time about it because we're starting to sound like our parents sometimes, but yet we don't really see that.

DI: You know, you see your life at sixteen years old and then being young and having children, and then kids grow up and are teenagers, and the whole soul-searching with what you want to do. They're such different stages in your life – so the trick is to move together in those phases. He went on the Camino for a month – in my opinion there's nothing better for our marriage than him hiking with our daughter. I mean, what great bonding between my daughter and him. So sometimes I think it's really healthy to be apart, and we still do that, in our own way, on a day-to-day basis. Not enough, though. I think we need to do it more.

BR: You trying to tell me something!?

DI: I think it's important to maintain your individuality in the relationship.

BR: I agree. When I think back, I think that Diana and I grew up in a time when it was definitely different then than it is now. There was this whole track – you go to school, you get educated, you get a job, you get married, you have kids, and that's what you do. And I look back at it now and I think, 'Whoever set this thing up?' You know? What the hell's that about? But that kind of set how our lives worked. We had a life together. We tried really hard so Diana didn't have to work all the time, because it was our view that Mum should be with the kids as much as she can. And that's how we grew up and that's how it was beat in our head. Everyone we associated with, that was their main driving force in life. That progression of life.

DI: But now we're at a point. This journey here in Edinburgh is going to end in ten months. And we're trying to come up with a plan for the future, and it's difficult. It's really difficult. We have different ideas about what we'd like to do, but we want to get away from what's expected. We have this idea – there's this school we know in Guatemala, in a real rural area, and you can help and volunteer there for six months or something. Or we would like to get a van and travel across the States and see the US. You know, we have different ideas. Fortunately, both of us are in the same frame of mind. We'd really like to do something different.

BR: That's the best part of it. In the journey I've had a partner I love who I've been able to take the journey with, and we still have a lot of journey ahead of us, which is pretty cool.

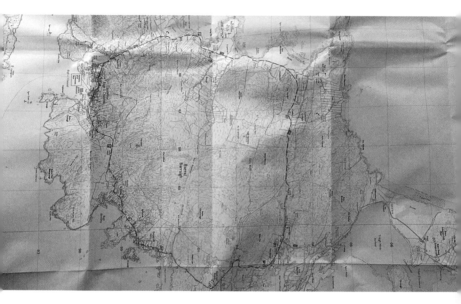

9. I Never Said, 'I Love You'

Three women are sharing. We all sit and listen, quietly nodding approval, giving space to their stories. I have meandered through the veins of the countryside, gently progressing along canal towpaths and bridleways, unobtrusively heading west towards a murmuring sun. The door shuts and my world contracts into an interior of smiles and laughter, comfort, tea and biscuits. In this home I find solidarity and friendship, a sense of belonging and being held.

.

L: I've never said to my mum, 'I love you,' and my mum has never said it to me. I know she loves me but I've never heard those words. My mum's eighty-three now so, you know, I don't know how much longer I'll have her. I mean, every time I leave her I give her a big cuddle, but I can't say those words.

I lost my dad six years ago. My dad was very much . . . he didn't show emotion – he was brought up that way, you know. At Christmas, New Year time, if I went to give him a cuddle, it was very much that I knew he didn't want me to give him a cuddle. So I wouldn't really say I cuddled him – I maybe put my arms around him, but I didn't cuddle him!

But I've always felt my mum wanted to show her feelings more. But she, again, was very old fashioned – she never did anything that would displease my dad because he was the boss. When my dad was here I never even got a cuddle from my mum. I would at Christmas or birthdays, but that would be it. But our relationship has changed, I think. It's like my mum is being more herself now that he's not there, much as she'd love still to have him there – but she is different. And my relationship with my mum is different, and we have a cuddle every time I leave her. But I just can't say these words. I don't know how she would react. I've heard her saying to my grandchildren, 'I love you,' and I was quite taken aback when I heard it. But I think that's more because they openly say, 'I love you.' I mean, I tell my grandchildren all the time, 'I love you.' I don't know – is that a generation thing, maybe?'

O: I had something similar in that my mum and dad were just the same as your mum and dad and they never, ever said, 'I love you.' I was the oldest, so that was the way I was too, because it would have been kind of embarrassing to be any other way. I don't know if by the time it got to my younger sister things may have been different because I was more or less out of the house all the time by then. After my mum died I'd never told her I loved her, and then my dad lived for another ten years. And there was a moment when I took him on the *Waverley* steamer that goes 'doon the watter'. And it was a lovely day out, and we were coming back and it was evening and the sky was lit up. It was glorious. As we came down the Clyde, my dad said, 'You know, I don't know how many more times I'm going to see this.' And I had this really weird feeling that now was the moment. If ever there was a moment, I should make it now because he was quite old. And I just could not change. I could not do it because he still hadn't done it. So I just sort of went, 'Aye, dad, aye.' There were no words.

L: But you said it without the words – by your body language, maybe?

O: Well, I think all of our lives growing up – it's about wee moments when you think, 'This must be the way they show love in that moment or this moment, but not in words.' So, yeah, I think that's as good as it gets.

M: I hear you both, and the reason that I probably became a therapist was because I was in therapy when I was twenty-eight. And it was just life that took me, and I ended up going to counselling. I thought I was going to go and speak about my mum because my mum had left me when I was two. Scottish people don't talk about their emotions, so I had been conditioned to not talk about how I felt for twenty-eight years of my life. So I felt, when I went to this therapy session, I was going to talk about my mum because she was a big issue. But the first words I can remember saying in my first-ever therapy session were, 'My dad never told me that he loved me.' I can remember hearing myself saying it and then thinking, 'What was all that about?' And the next three therapy sessions I just cried – for about three weeks! But the key thing that came out of that was that, obviously, my dad brought me and my three brothers up. And when he used to tuck me in bed at night he would say, 'Night, night. Who do you love the best?' And I would always say, 'You, Dad,' waiting for 'And I love you too.' But it never came. During the therapy I got angry, and this kept coming back and back and back. And my dad was still alive then, and I wrote my dad this letter and I actually posted it to him! So I suppose it was a love letter of sorts. He read this letter and then we had the conversation. But what he says to me is, 'You should know that I love you.' And I says, 'How should I know that you love me?' 'But you should know because you've always had the best of everything, so that's it.' So I had to come to the acceptance that I'm never going to hear it.

A couple of years later, I ended up having my son. So I chose that my son would hear that every day of his life. I was determined that every day he would hear 'I love you.' And I can remember, not long after we moved here, my dad was here every day, and he just loved my son, Ryan. You know, you'd just get in from work and Dad was here! It was one day after work and Ryan jumped up – he was only about three or something like that – and he got my cheeks and said, 'Oh, I just love you, Mum. I love you.' And my dad burst out crying. Then he said, 'That's what you meant.' I said, 'That's what I meant.' But the key thing was he still didn't say it. He still couldn't say 'I love you.' But at least I knew then that he knew what I meant. But I suppose we've got a choice, at the end of the day. At least I know that I've broken that cycle, that I had the choice to go one way or the other. I know he loved me and I know he still loves me – wherever he is. But I knew then, when I saw it in his eyes, that he didn't understand what love was.

L: What if my mum passes and I've never said it? I don't know about the other way – the regret if she doesn't say it – but I know, if I don't tell my mum I love her, I'll regret it.

O: Well, my dad died just shortly after that trip on the *Waverley* steamer, unexpectedly, from a heart attack. And so I would say, I know there's a blockage there – I couldn't do it. I wasn't really prepared to do it, but I think if you want to make a breakthrough, you maybe need to think about it before and know that you're going to do it. But steel yourself because it's not going to come first. You're going to have to make a breakthrough for you – so you feel better for the rest of your life.

10. We're Just Humans on This Rock

It feels cold, even though the sun is bright and warm this morning. I am beginning to feel that pulse of journeying, that enduring rhythm of movement and of being – the 'sacred drift' that allows space and time to ease gently in and out of moments. I am hearing a little more clearly, limping a little less. My shoulders ache, but only in passing. We sit on a bench and talk as the world rouses itself. A church bell tolls in the distance, welcoming.

I'm just trying to think about when I've had that moment, that spark. I've had it once, once I would say, with a girl. And it's a girl I used to go out with – about six years ago now. I met her in a nightclub and we just started dancing together. And I remember straightaway just spinning her. We were doing this really cheesy dancing. I was spinning her and tipping her over and things like that. Straightaway, you know you have that connection with someone. And it's just comfortable, and you can hold their hand and it's not awkward. It's like we've been doing it for years. And I always remember that on that first night I met her, it was like that. We were just so comfortable together.

So like six weeks later we were engaged. I asked her to marry me because I was just so in love with her. I was like, 'She's the one.' But then it fell apart – which was sad. It makes me feel sad. And it's a regret of mine as well. Maybe there are things I could have done better. Maybe I was a bit stupid as well. I always look back and think. I remember there was a night out and she wanted me to go over to her friends and I never went. Or I was meant to go and meet her gran for dinner and I never went. And I think it was because I was hungover from the night before as well, which was really annoying. Maybe, if I had put in more effort with wee things like that, we might have still been together. Maybe not.

She finished with me because she didn't feel the same any more. Fair enough – that happens with people. I was working long hours but still being stupid and going out with my friends. She had problems as well. I guess it was the wrong time. It's one of those moments you regret. I can see now, if I met someone like that now, I think it would be completely different.

I'm changed from what I was. I've become quite political about stuff and I get quite angry about things. I decided I wanted to do something about it and I really got into photography. And I kinda found my voice through photography. I decided that's how I'm going to show my message and help people – by doing this.

There's such a negative atmosphere about migrants coming here. The words they use like 'invading' and 'swarming', and it's always just a figure and it's a number and it's a cost. But they're just people. They're humans. So my idea for a project was to take photos – just normal photos of these people and show them as humans. A lot of people are struggling with life and they're looking for reasons why that is. And you look in the paper and you're being told it's because of migrants. They get that anger towards them. My whole idea for the project is to counteract this atmosphere. It's the yin and the yang. I want to be on the other side, showing this positive light – if I can, if I'm good enough. Maybe I'll print a book and see what it looks like. Hopefully, people will see it and maybe change their opinion of migrants – the idea that they're a problem and they're ruining our country and they're costing our society. 'Cause they're not – they're helping our society.

I always feel there's a stereotype. People think that they're coming here and stealing our benefits. But if you speak to migrants, they all say, 'Well, I'm applying for this job,' or 'I'm hoping to study this.' They're all really eager to come here and contribute and live their lives. They're just women and children. They just happen to stand on a rock over there that has a different name from our rock.

They say that Scotland was the last of the free, and it's because of the Picts – they were so communal together, they used to live together. They would help each other. You know there's evidence of that. There should be more of this community spirit. There should be more compassion. In politics especially there should be more compassion. It should be just about compassion and love for each other. We're just humans on this rock.

11. 'I Love You, But I'm Scared'

Thank you for sharing this pain, my friend, for exposing the wound, for letting me glimpse your tender heart. On another day, in another place, we might sit and laugh together and talk beneath the blossom.

•

It was on our anniversary. I woke up and she was crying. She says, 'I'm scared.'

'What do you mean, scared?'

She says to me, 'I love you, but I'm scared.'

I said, 'Don't be scared – there's still a lot of life to be lived. You'll be here, you'll be fine. You did us proud.'

I'd booked up a holiday and everything else as a surprise for her. We never got to the holiday. She only lasted six months and that was it. On her deathbed she looked round to everybody gathered there, and she turned around to me and said, 'I love you,' shut her eyes, and that was it. I'll never forget that. I'll never forget it. The love I lack is unbearable, to be honest. And I'm not coping, to be honest. I'm not. How to cope? Where to start, where to start? The journal, I'll go back to my journal. And reading it, you were unhappy – no, wait, wait, you were happy too, you were happy too.

12. After a Wee While, We Started To Notice Each Other

Bright skies. The clouds hang high, gently moving to the west, to the sea. I'm searching for your door amongst many doors. I am tired and a little anxious. Inside, there is a welcome and hugs and tea and breakfast, from 'long lost friends' I've never met before.

•

M: We were both part of L'Arche community in Liverpool. Maria had gone there in July '78 and I'd been in the community in Kent for two years before that. And then I moved to Liverpool. I arrived at this Victorian house in the middle of the night. And the person who had brought me up in the van said, 'Oh, I'll show you around the house.' And he showed me round the house in the dark because it was midnight, you see. So I went with him and he said, 'Well, here's your room.' And I opened the door and there was this kind of lifeless shape in front of the window. And I got into bed and then this lifeless shape moved and muttered, 'Oh, fuck!' And then I went to sleep. And the next morning the door opened and I thought, 'I don't know what to expect here,' you know, because there's people with learning difficulties here. Then this tongue appeared from behind the door, followed by this woman with Down's Syndrome. And she said, 'I've brought you a cup of coffee.' And I thought, 'Ah, wonderful.' And then, after a wee while, probably about six to eight years, Maria and I started to notice each other!

MA: In a different way, yes, we did. Mike had been away over in the States for about three months. During that time I had led the community. Not long after he came back, we had a community weekend, where we were kind of looking forward to the year ahead. And basically, Mike's experience of the weekend was that Sue and I had sewed it up, and he wasn't very pleased about this!

M: At the community weekend it emerged that Maria was Assistant Community Leader, and Sue had done a private deal with you, so I was kind of carrying the torch for justice for the community, you see!

MA: Oh right, OK.

M: So we went out from that meeting and we went for a long stomping walk when you told me everything that was wrong with me. I told you everything that was wrong with you. And then we realised we loved each other!

MA: It wasn't quite as simple as that! You know, when there was conflict with Mike and me – and there was quite considerable conflict between us – what happened was when we stopped to talk we began to hear each other's story.

M: I told my story to you in a way that I probably had never spoken about before. And you told your story to me. So we kind of said, 'This seems to be really important – let's continue to share at this kind of level.' That was the point of transformation. And then Maria fell down a bank.

MA: I was doing a mock walkabout!

M: And she fell down a bank! And I thought, 'Anybody who can do that is just wonderful.' She was showing off and she disappeared. She was trying to be sophisticated!

MA: No good at it! I knew Mike quite well before this, but only then did we actually begin to listen to each other's deeper story. That's really what happened, and the conflict initiated that. But it was actually the walk, and the walks that we did subsequently, that allowed that to flourish. I mean, at a certain point that changed, from recognising the need to listen to each other's story to recognising that we actually had begun to fall in love with each other. And that was walking along Holly Road.

M: 'Cause I had decided that I would never get married. You know, I'd come from quite a violent home. And I wanted that to stop with me, and I didn't want it to continue. But with Maria I thought, 'Ah well, I should ask her to marry me.' So I was thinking about all these romantic places. But we were on a train, from London to Liverpool Lime Street, and there came a moment, I think, when we were going into a tunnel. I just said, 'Maria, would you ever think about marrying me?' I said, 'You know, you can go off and think about that 'cause you'll probably need a bit of time with that question.' And she just said, 'Yes,' and I said, 'What!' So we went and we got this plastic half-bottle of wine to celebrate.

MA: Suddenly it was as if we belonged together. That's what had happened. There was the sexual connection, which is really strong. But there's also that sense of belonging.

M: By this time I had moved down to London and I was studying. Maria was still in Liverpool. So I'd ring Maria relatively late at night and she would be almost incoherent because she was so tired, you know, and I just got so impatient with that. So then we thought, 'OK, we'll try early in the morning.' So we started phoning each other in the morning, and that was just as bad! At this point I was staying in a Benedictine monastery. And then, suddenly, I start getting all these letters.

MA: I just found the phone calls to Mike impossible. But I was also conscious that we weren't building a connection terribly well. Anyway, I got sick. And I got so sick that the doctor said I needed to be away for two weeks. There's an urban monastery in Crosby, and I went and stayed there. And I had this most fantastic room and I just looked out on the woods and watched the squirrels. You know, I had time to be alone and in myself. And I began to think, 'Where can I give some space to our relationship that is in the context of where we are living.' I knew that in the afternoon I had a couple of hours, so I started to write letters to Mike about what was important about our relationship, our life, our love together.

M: It was quite powerful in terms of receiving them.

MA: From those letters we distilled what was important for us, and we developed a charter for our marriage. And we look at that, usually once a year.

M: And then the other thing that we decided we would do, just before getting married, was a thirty-day retreat together in silence. I think it meant that in learning to be silent together, we learnt who each other was at a different level.

MA: It's about that ongoing noticing of one another.

You know when you listen to a piece of music, I'm thinking Beethoven's Pastoral Symphony, I'm thinking chords in Dvořák's New World Symphony, that I just love. And I don't know why I love them, but I love them. When we retell our story and we're telling it in a way that we're being listened to, both with each other and other people, it's like hearing that music again. That's what it is for me.

13. I'm Not the Most Eloquent

A rest day of sorts. I have some time to relax and think before the journey continues. Time to write, to plan, to connect with folk at home. Irn-Bru flirts with me – the sugar, the preservatives, are tempting me. A beguiling orange thing of beauty! A fizzing, irresistible explosion of sparkle. I will resist!

•

I'm not the most eloquent when I talk about emotions. I can talk about anything else – football or golf or anything where I can stand on my own pontification. There's a few different chapters to my love story. I get tearful when I start thinking about it. It started about thirty years ago. There's a lot of water under the bridge after all these years. It's been smooth and tranquil, other times rough and stormy. But, thankfully, we held hands throughout those times and we got through it.

I have four different parts to my love story, actually. The first was when Ryan was born. We tried to have him for a long time and eventually he came along – it was good fun practising, to be fair! He eventually came along after we'd been to doctors and hospitals and nurses. I had to drop my trousers in front of doctors. They tested me out and things like that, but eventually we got there! And now he's going to university, our work's done and he's heading off into the big world.

The second story was when I had my brain tumour. And I'd suffered from depression and anxiety for years and years, thinking it was me. But once the brain tumour was removed, I sort of became a different person again. I became more like the person I once was – fun-loving, good-looking, all those things. But Maureen was there all the time, helping me through.

The third story was the love for the two doctors I had to see. The surgeon, known as X. I don't know what the X stood for – it might have been Xavier or something. A wee, tiny man but a lovely, lovely man. And a Dr Walker. He actually diagnosed me when I went to the hospital. I went into Emergency one night, and it was like premature dementia I was having. I was getting really forgetful and things like that. And he just nailed it there and then, really. He sent me for scans, and then everything else happened from there.

So after twenty-five years of marriage – and that's the fourth love story – we're still going strong -ish! There's a lot of love, compassion and learning: how to give each other space and to grow individually and as a family. And finally, just to prove I can remember my wedding vows: 'Love is patient, love is kind, it does not envy, it does not boast, it is not proud, it is not rude, it is not self-seeking, it is not easily angered and does not keep record of wrongs.'

14. It's Starting To Come Together

I gaze at mirrored surfaces of water that reflect the fractured light of the broken sky above. It is grey and I am cold for the first time. I have too much to carry somehow and my clothes are the wrong clothes! I do not feel comfortable. Your silhouette approaches. Someone is whistling a joyfully unfamiliar tune.

•

I actually lived at Eton College because my stepfather taught there, so I think I was probably there when Cameron was there, maybe when Boris was there. I actually went to a different school for over-privileged children! Yeah, because my dad's family had a tradition of private schooling. To sum it up, I think these places have excellent staff, excellent facilities, but it's still a very strange place to be, and it took me a good while to get used to boarding. And it was quite a shock suddenly, at the age of thirteen, to be sharing a dormitory with strangers. Also, at that stage, my folks' marital status was pretty rough. My mum says she remembers me as a very anxious boy. I think it did tighten me up actually –

and it did close me down to a lot of things. And I found it very difficult to relate to people, really. When I was at this public school, there was this chap that I didn't know very well. He'd come to the school at a later stage, I think, at the age of sixteen or seventeen, and he was Malaysian. I think he'd come from a much more relaxed environment, much more relaxed than an English public school! Everything was always a bit stressful there, but once he just touched me on the shoulder and it struck me that no one had ever done that before, certainly not at that school!

At university, I'd come out of this public school world and I found so many people were just 'ill-mannered oiks'! But then I met my lovely Greek girlfriend and she brought that kind of Greek culture and warmth. I really relaxed and certainly opened up after that.

I'm actually at quite an exciting stage of my life. I'm convinced that I caught the Chinese flu in 1993. For twenty-three years I had a big problem with this mysterious fatigue, which was described as ME or chronic fatigue syndrome. Just the last eighteen months, really, I've been making a steady recovery. I've started to exercise again. I've been working part-time for most of my working life because of the fatigue, but I think I might be ready to start working full-time again quite soon. It has affected my personal life, but I'm feeling more confident now. So, yeah, I'd like to meet someone and settle down. I didn't think it was possible that anyone would want to be with someone who spent most of the time in bed, sleeping! Loneliness has been a major feature, really. The feeling that no one really understands your situation is a horrible feeling. It was a little bit sore because I know that even close friends and family must have been tapping their heads behind my back, because conventional medical science was still doubting the existence of a medical problem. It is recognised now as a medical as opposed to a psychological problem. And I had a medical test that showed what was going on in my blood. I call that test result my 'Sanity Certificate'! A few close friends and family do understand now, and that's very reassuring.

I really feel so lucky. I'm in my dream job now. I actually started as a volunteer for the best part of a year. At the Christmas do there were a few short speeches just thanking the volunteers, but John singled me out because I had 'really blossomed', and I felt that I had come out and blossomed! My health was improving and I felt like I was in exactly the right place. I certainly feel a lot more at ease with myself and everyone around me now.

I can see now actually in my dad, who is no longer with us, and my stepfather, who had very similar backgrounds in British public schools – they both found it very difficult to relate to people. It came out in different ways, but I think in this current generation we've been allowed to relax and we've been allowed to be ourselves a lot more. It's starting to come together, I think! It's only been forty-six years!

15. What's the Problem?

I am sitting, listening. I don't have any words or thoughts of reassurance; I have not been where you have been, my friend. I hope you take my silence as an offering of solidarity, of abiding. It is night outside. A street lamp flickers. My eyes are growing heavy with sleep, I sink deeper into my chair, warmth enveloping me like a blanket.

•

'What's the problem?' and he says, 'I need to get to the toilet from the bed and I'm getting measured for a walking stick. So they're going to send someone out and they're going to measure me and then they're going to measure my stick. And then they're going to order it from the hospital. Then they're going to do this and that and . . .' I'm thinking, 'That'll take ages!' I remember him saying, from twenty years ago, that he'd been up the lakes, and things like this, and he went on about this walking stick. It was all carved and beautiful, and he described it in perfect detail. So, I thought, he'd probably want something like that. I thought I'd get up early the next day and go through to Edinburgh. I hunted up the High Street. I walked everywhere – I couldn't find the one he was after. And I was just about to go home when I saw this barbershop. I went in there and I had a look at all their things and I found this perfect one! I thought, 'That's brilliant!'

So I came home, gave it to him and he just burst into tears. And I thought, 'I don't understand this because it's only a walking stick.' But the fact that I'd spent the whole day looking for it, came back at five o'clock at night, gave it to him so he could get from the bed to the toilet. He was just so grateful.

But he could only use it for three days, and that was him.

16. Nothing Short of Love

I find my way through the city, across roads, down alleys, to the river. To the south I can see Govan, home of GalGael – a place of inspiration and activism, where love takes root deeply, grounded into the fabric of the community. As I cross the Clyde, a rainbow greets my arrival amidst the sunshine and showers. I am here.

·

One of the things that always surprises me in here is that the word 'safe' comes up so many times when people express what matters to them about this space! And I've always thought, 'Safe? How can it be safe?' There's a machine shop, there are chainsaws, there are people with previous convictions around murder. How can it be safe? And I think, for me, it's connected to a sense that you can make mistakes, that you're not going to be cast out for making mistakes. There's a kind of sense of acceptance.

This is a community of solidarity; there's something really powerful in that.

GalGael's story starts at the Pollok Free State. We started

around the campfire at one of the motorway camps, protesting about the building of the M77. And that was started by Colin really in response to seeing something happen to the woods that he grew up in. He started going down and doing tree-sits. He did a tree-sit up an ash tree for nine days. He was up a crane for three days. And then he decided to carve an eagle totem pole. And he made a poster for an event that he was going to hold – a big rave in the woods. And through that he got enough bodies down to lift this eagle totem pole and set it in the ground.

It was probably on and off before that point – but, after that, I think people started camping there every day. It was a really difficult space. You regularly had people coming in and drinking lots round the fire, taking Jellies and carrying knives, so it was really quite a dangerous place. During the time we were down there, there were three near-deaths. I think about it quite regularly because I think there is still learning coming out of that experience.

I suppose one of the turning points was the first near-death incident in the camp. There were a lot of people down there one night because there was a rumour going round that The Hothouse Flowers were going to be playing – so the whole wood was totally crowded with people, with no lights whatsoever. And this big fight kicked off. This woman, who was down there with her kids, got hit on the head with a hammer. And that's when there was this really big learning experience of what freedom means, what it takes to create freedom. That it isn't just about the exercising of free will – it's about taking responsibility for one another's wellbeing. We managed to get through all of that, and so many other hurdles.

But when the road went through, we thought, 'We don't

want to throw away all this learning.' So that's when we decided that we were going to create an organisation as a vehicle to take that forward. To move from what we didn't want, which was a road and childhood asthma and pollution and the local community being cut off from the parkland. And move to what we did want, which I still find really hard to put into words! I think it's hard to put into words because it's so big, in some ways. I think, for me, it's something around lives well lived. Instead of lives wasted.

GalGael turned twenty last Friday, and it has caused us to have quite a period of reflection. What are we? Who are we? What matters to us? And to spend quite a bit of time really poring over that. The last point we are coming to agreement on is our purpose. And I really struggle to put that into words that feel broad enough but not too vague. So we've basically ended up with some form of wording that includes 'bringing greater humanity and love to our public lives and collective work'. And what's been really interesting is how people have responded to those words, particularly 'love'. People have sort of been saying, 'That's too fluffy – we're not fluffy.' A lot of people were saying things like, 'I'm not sure if I'm too happy with that.' I think also they were probably doubting that it was a genuine offer: 'Can I really believe that there is something that is genuinely offered here, or is it that kind of false love?' There was a fear there, almost. And then the discussion kind of came to the point of saying, 'Well, that's what our times call for – nothing short of love.'

17. There's More *Amour* in It

Amongst the comfortable clutter of paint pots and brushes we chat, sitting deep in leather chairs. Sounds of breakfast and conversation murmuring behind me, children painting, the day stirring outside. The distant sound of a car horn. Paint pots flying, fingers dipped in yellow.

·

We met at a gig, probably two years before we actually started going out. I was in a relationship; I'd been married for seven or eight years and we were living in Cheshire. But all my work was in Glasgow, so I used to drive up and down, and up and down – and things weren't going very well. My ex had really bad depression, but then we had our daughter and that was a reason to stay together. But I don't think either of us were happy at that point. I would drive up to Glasgow and stay in cheap B&Bs for a few nights. I had my company and the company was doing fairly well. Then I would drive home, and every time I drove home, more often than not, it would cross my mind to drive the car off the road.

Around this time I'd made a music video for a band and they had their first single launch at King Tut's. After the gig Stephanie was there, outside, with her flatmate, who was a journalist. Stephanie had come along with her to review this band's live gig. There's an all-night drinking bar open till four in the morning, so we decided to all troop along there. We sat talking and it ended up just me and Stephanie. I told her I was married and had a daughter. She had a daughter too and they were the same age. And we ended up talking for the rest of the night, just the two of us. In the early morning we said goodbye but she, being ever the businesswoman, left me with a list of all the therapies that she did. She gave me her number too, and that was it for probably nearly another two years.

Two years later we're on Facebook and a friend of mine, Francis, had written something and Stephanie had replied. And I thought, 'That's the same Stephanie I met two years ago.' So I sent her a Facebook message and a friend request saying, 'You're who I met two years ago at the gig.' She said 'Yes' and then friended me on Facebook. And then, that Christmas, my wife at the time said that she thought that we should split up. And I was like, 'Ah, thank God,' because I thought that if I left her, then she would kill herself. The Facebook messages with Stephanie carried on and the comments carried on. There was something there, but I was too nervous. I'd been in a relationship for seventeen years – it's a long time and I hadn't been out in the world, as it were.

For our first proper date she took me to a life-drawing class, where I found myself drawing a naked man for most of the evening. She said she didn't know it was going to be a man! It was not long after that I realised that I'd never been in love before.

I thought I'd been in love before, but it wasn't until I met her that I realised I never had been. What I felt with her was totally different – it was totally different from every relationship I had ever had. Around that time I was filming a series on love – I'd been filming that all over Scotland. I was filming all these people who were claiming to be in love and I was thinking, 'You're not in love – your life's a lie,' because that's what I'd been through. Although it was really lovely to do, still I was thinking, 'No, you're not really in love.' I thought the whole love thing was a fantasy.

Whenever I see her – this is now our eighth year – whenever I see her, I'm excited to see her! I'd never experienced that before. And we argue all the time. We have the most blazing rows, mainly 'cause of her – she instigates them! But I'd never had those kind of rows and those arguments before with people. And I think that might be part of it. There's more passion in it, there's more energy in it, there's more *more* in it, there's more *amour* in it!

I thought there must be so many people who go through relationships where they're just in it because they think they should be in it, and I think that's what I was doing before. The reason I was in it seventeen years with my ex was because I thought that's what I have to do. I thought I had to get married at some point and have children at some point. It just became the next step. I remember my company was going through a bad patch and my daughter had been born and was going to school and my ex had made it clear she didn't want any more children. I had just turned forty, I had a new car, I had a really good pension, I was miserable and I had bookmarked on my computer natural burial sites because I thought that was my next thing. Isn't that weird? You're told this is what you're supposed to do, this is how it should be, and for me, at that time, everything was how it should be.

Just seeing people on the street, seeing people together, seeing families together, I'd look around and think, 'How many people are just doing it because they think they have to do it, and they'd be much happier if they weren't?' So I went from a nice house in Cheshire – new car, nice pension, company doing well – to a couple of years later with Stephanie, having nothing, the company gone, the car was getting older, the ex-wife had the house. Sometimes I'd have just £10 for the week – but I was so happy.

18. Who Are You Waiting For?

We met just yesterday on the path and today we meet again in the rain. We search in vain for a place to be comfortable. Eventually we settle between the entrance and the toilets of a high street café, discreetly hidden from the cashiers because we are not buying. I am not buying. Not today!

·

I was actually adopted from birth in Canada. My adopted parents both passed away quite a while back now, but it was some of their relatives who said, 'Why don't we research the family name?' And the family name, McCulloch, was fascinating — they're a bunch of tyrants!

The main McCulloch was a real piece of work. I mean he was the equivalent of a pirate and a thief, and the rest of it. And it was after that that I thought, 'I really want to know about my roots,' so I tracked down my mother through the adoption agency in Canada and after a few years I managed to make the connection. I was in my mid thirties. After some time she finally got back to me and we started sending letters. It was New Year's Day eight years ago and I got this phone call, and it was 'Hello, is that Rory?' It was my mum from Canada! Never spoken to her before in my life.

I was staying in Glasgow at the time and she tracked me down – she had spoken to my ex-partner in Helensburgh. So she had already got a bit of background about me, and because of that she was quite confident. For me, I was kind of taken aback. But we just spoke as if we'd known each other for years. At the time it was so easy and so natural I didn't think about it. It was just a buzz. It was a case of 'This is my mother!' It wasn't until I put the phone down that I went into absolute shock for about two weeks. I thought, 'I'm in my mid thirties and I've only just spoken to my mum for the first time.' And my head exploded. I really went into meltdown.

Don't get me wrong, my family, my mum and dad I had grown up with, they were my parents – that was it. My adopted mother, Jo, had suggested, in my late teens, did I want to get in touch with my birth mum? It just felt at the time it wasn't the right time.

I actually met my mum for the first time, and my half-sister, in June last year. They came over to meet me here in Scotland. I was at the airport waiting for them. I was there for ages and all the taxi drivers were asking, 'Who are you waiting for?' I explained and the word got round and they were like, 'Oh, you're meeting your mum for the first time – that's amazing!' Eventually, there they were. A quick hug with my sister. My mum came over and said, 'How are you doing?' And I was totally in shock. And she said, 'Right, so what are we doing?' And it was as if I hadn't really got past the airport bit, to be honest! Most of the time you have that instant recognition – or I had assumed so. But she was quite short and I didn't see the similarities. We both were very tense about it so we didn't go too deep. We kept it safe.

It wasn't until I saw them two months later in Canada, because we'd already broken the ice, that we kind of relaxed. I had a ball, an absolute ball. And it was the husband I was worried about. I thought he might find me quite intrusive because they have three kids of their own. But he was a superstar. And their friends came over, and no one knew about me except for four people, so I was meeting their family for the first time and they had never heard or understood who I was. But they were all so accommodating, and it was just the friendliest and the warmest holiday I've ever had. There was this realisation that I've got another family now.

I'd been quite self-sufficient, so getting close to people in that kind of way was quite unusual for me. But they were saying, 'No, you're part of the family now.' I was thinking, 'Really?' It is one of those things that is difficult to put into words but it means so much. It was so out of the context of what I could understand or describe, but it was so much deeper at the same time. It was a grounding feeling, a deep feeling, very subtle, if you like, almost like you're walking on a substance, but just above it there's something there that ties everything together. I don't know, just a sense of wholeness or completeness. Up until that point there was a gap – just something that I needed to find out or connect to.

I suppose going to Canada was a big deal for me because I'd not been out there for twenty years. I managed to go to the house where I grew up, and across the road from that was the church where my adoptive mother was buried. That was quite a surreal moment. It took me ages to find her and I started getting in a real panic. 'I know it's here somewhere!' And then, eventually, I did find it and it was like, 'Phew.' It was so strange because while I was there, my birth mother, Liz, and her husband were happily walking, taking in the view on a lovely, lovely day in this graveyard beside the coast. They were with me, just loving the view and respecting the moment.

19. Let's Keep It Brief

I am journeying with the canal, moving along the water's edge, idly marking my steps to the flurries of the wind on the water. Impulsive, bright, laconic and almost indiscernible, you tell me the things of your heart in the damp drizzle. These 'things' amount to just four words, which puncture my romanticism. A moment of you, casually thrown.

•

My love story?

House, dog, marriage, baby. In that order.

20. Everything's Fine

Glasgow feels wonderful today. Full of humour, garrulous and fun. It is all noise and motion and pop. Perched on a corner, I am watching the crowds pass me by. Like a perfectly choreographed film, they criss-cross endlessly before me, Fred Astaire waiting in the wings for the final flourish! I feel the faintest gnawing inside – the urge to continue the journey, the need for bigger skies.

·

I went to Skyros, the Greek island, in 1998, and that had a profound impact on me. I remember we were in Atsitsa and we had to walk to town, and it was quite a walk and I was tired. It was hot and I got a bit lost. There's a church and a monastery, and it was about five o'clock at night. And I went up to the pretty bit on the top with the blue skies and I saw there were some lamps and paraffin, and I thought, 'Yeah, yeah, yeah, this is OK, and whatever.' And then I walked down and went into the church, which was darker. But when I was there I saw this light and it felt as though I was in the presence of God. And this light entered my body and it just felt like a divine love. And when I walked out of that place my whole world had changed, and it was as though this love was just there, and it felt amazing. Safe, secure, maybe? It's almost as though there's this infinity, a nothingness and a being-ness – and almost, after that, death didn't scare me. That sort of feeling. Quite a heightened awareness as well. Bliss is how you might describe it, but it was more than just a moment of bliss. I suppose it was a fundamental change in trust, faith – not in a 'religious' sense but in a sense of 'everything's fine'.

The way I would maybe describe how I was before was 'a bit brittle'. There was a strong protection. So I might have appeared to be strong but it would have been easy to break. That whole Skyros experience softened me so I could bend in the wind or bend in the breeze. Now, maybe it's about me being me, rather than being who other people maybe expect. I'm also feeling a bit more true to myself. When I was younger, having experiences with guys, I didn't know how to say to people, 'Bugger off!', 'Get lost!', 'Take a hike!' So I was quite, you know, the good girl, the people-pleaser type. Not that my mother was that way at all – she's very advanced in terms of feminism and doing her stuff. So I'm not sure where that came from. It wasn't from my mum or my dad. It's not being more selfish. It's actually being more true to myself and feeling able to say, 'This isn't working for me.' When I left my last job, it's the first time I haven't just said, 'I'm going.' You know, hand my notice in and 'I'm off.' I had a conversation with my boss and she was really good. And I tried other stuff like compressing my hours, doing different things. And I'm really glad I did that because it felt as though I was finally becoming an adult and able to say how I felt about things.

I also think work and relationships are quite, for me, related. There's something there. You're in a relationship with your job, your career, whatever it is you're doing, and that's where my relationship has been, and maybe at the expense of my social life and personal life. I've created a space for myself now to have a bit more fun, a bit more time and a bit more enjoyment. The word that came to mind was 'liberation'. And, for me, it's allowing myself to feel that, to really feel it and to go with it, which maybe I've held down. And I've been in a relationship which is very much based on need and dependency, and that's the opposite of what I think love should be. You're choosing, almost every day, every moment, whether it's a place, a person, whatever it is – it's a freedom of choice to be there. So love's almost as though that all drops away and there's moments of, I suppose, connection. Yeah, connection is the thing. Connection.

21. Dashing Good Looks

Security. A home full of 'stuff', safe amongst the objects. On the path I have my rucksack, full of 'important' stuff, pockets bulging! Safe amongst these objects too. I carry the burden every day. It journeys with me wherever I am. I stop, leaving the bag behind for just a moment, and feel the weightless freedom, without a pang of regret.

•

She set us a task: name five things you love about yourself. So I did that in the morning, and the house was silent and I said, 'Right, five things I love about me.' And I couldn't find one. And I wrote on the postcard, 'I cannae think of one, never mind five.' It would be easier to think of five things I don't love about myself – it's not my dashing good looks! I just couldn't think of anything. Everybody else could think of stuff and were reading out their things like 'sense of humour'. But I didn't connect that to love. Now I wouldn't say I love my sense of humour because a lot of people can't wait to see the back of me because of my sense of humour. Aye, I could've put that down, but I didn't connect it. To me, love's a different thing. Again, it's the way you've been brought up. My mum and dad weren't lovey-dovey. My dad, I would say, aye, he's more lovey-dovey than my mum. My mum was like, 'Can you get off me?' kind of thing. 'Don't kiss me!' and just shrugging him off all the time. You tend to take a lot off your parents because they're really who you look up to when you're growing up, and they kind of tune you in for the rest of your life. So they've a lot to answer for, the two of them, I can tell you that. Look at the state of me now.

But for the first fifty years of my life I just sat in this room and I never said a word. Now I tend to shove myself a wee bit forward. Which is why I lost my voice! Cancer is never a good thing, but you've got to take positives through the negatives. And to me, I'm six years down the line now, since I got this. The first year was terrible – I had no voice at all. Then I eventually got my voice and I've not shut up since!

I've got an awful bad habit of going off the rails, alcohol-wise. I've always had a problem with alcohol. Ever since I had my first pint, me and alcohol didn't get on. I try my best to stay on the straight and narrow – but it's no' easy, eh? There was one day I fell off the wagon. The following night I read back my journal to the days I was feeling good. And I saw the thoughts I had. If I'd read that, I would not have taken that drink. And now, before I go drinking, I read my journal. It gives me a bit of strength. Aye, you've got the choice up until you buy the drink, but once you've bought the drink it's too late. But you've always got that choice.

Life's a learning process. And I'm still in a nappy stage. I thought I was a big human being, aye, so I did. I didn't care nothing. I'm prepared to learn. That's the good thing.

22. And the Music Went, and the Music Went, and the Music Went!

Scotland, rearing up thrillingly, the graceful fells before me. You welcome me and my companions at the door and we go into your world of dance and warmth. Lounging in your sofa seems the most glorious pastime. Coffee, snacks and your stories weaving together, like the tango you so longed to dance.

•

J: We did meet at a dance, didn't we?

W: I was brought up in Helensburgh. There were two tennis clubs, and one ran a Saturday dance for a long, long time, which I used to go to after having a few pints in the pub. And this girl I knew, who came from Balloch, which is over the hill, used to come with some friends. And this time she had a new friend with her, and this just happened to be Jenny. I danced with her a few times. And a few weeks later I phoned up Hazel and said, 'That cousin of yours – how can I get in touch with her?' And she gave me her contact details, and I phoned her up. And I said, 'It's Willie – we met at the dance the other night.' She said, 'Willie who?' I said, 'The fellow with the beard.'

J: I couldn't remember!

W: And then we arranged to go out. There were one or two ups and downs, but that's how we came to be together.

J: We went to ballroom dancing classes. We longed to dance the tango. We really wanted to dance the tango! And the dance teacher – he kept standing on my toes. He kept saying, 'You're just not moving your feet out of the way. It's your fault!' So we kind of gave it up, didn't we?

W: Yes, yes, aha.

J: But we were circle dancers before that.

W: One of the things I didn't like about it was that they did a wee bit of different dances, and you didn't have a chance, in my view, to absorb it. It was the samba, and they said, 'Listen for the beat and start when you're ready.' So I shut my eyes and the music went, and the music went, and the music went! Then the music stopped and we were still standing there!

J: Waiting for the beat.

W: I'd say I've got cloth ears.

J: I always loved dancing. Willie and I were both keen dancers. And you know, if it's a ballroom dancing situation, he would go off and ask other people to dance and I'd be sitting there like a lemon, having to wait for a man to come and ask me to dance. So when I went circle dancing, I thought, 'That's wonderful.' You just dance! You don't need a partner; if you want to dance, you just join the circle and dance. Now, not every circle dance teacher starts the way I teach. We start off and we do the dance called 'Give Yourself to Love'. Then we have a quiet moment when I say things like, 'Let's think about the energy of the earth beneath our feet, and let's think about the energy of the sky above our heads. And let's think about that sky energy and that earth energy meeting in us and then being shared around the circle. And at that point we are holding hands so that energy is being brought all the way round the circle. For me – I don't know about anyone else – but for me, I get this vision of a ribbon of energy going about the room, going round the circle, connecting people.

The group that dances with me every week, they're very happy coming along, being part of the group. Belonging – there's a 'belonging' thing in there. They feel embraced by the group, I think. You know, they all look after each other. It's a very healing thing.

23. I Love the Bones of Them

Along the river, the birds hum their choral songs, calling in the sky, bidding the sun goodnight, welcoming the moon. We are walking. Past lads fishing, through swathes of wild garlic, amongst the rhododendrons and the fairy trees.

.

I've always been a bit of an island. I've always kept myself to myself. After I had Ellis, I ended up with really bad postnatal depression. It wasn't just 'I'm a bit depressed', I was terrified of everything. If I saw a plane, I saw it explode in the sky. If I saw a tree, I saw it fall down. If I was walking up the road with a pram, I saw a car hit the pram. It was the fact that these things were so real to me – they didn't feel like hallucinations. But that's what they were. And I think it was compounded by the fact that I really wanted to breastfeed, and they really push it and I couldn't do it. You are seen to be a failure. And I was looking around at everyone, thinking, 'But they can all do it. Why can't I do it?' And somehow I worked it up to, 'Well, I can't love him enough.' Even though I loved him more than anything. I just couldn't imagine loving anything more.

We ended up in hospital with 'failure to thrive'. He was born at five pounds eleven. He was five pounds three when he left, but they were happy with that. I remember going to the doctor for myself when he was seven weeks old and the doctor ignored me and said, 'Can I have a look at the baby?' And he weighed him and he was four pounds. The whole time I'd been told, 'Keep on, keep on, keep on,' but what had happened is my milk hadn't come in. After that, I couldn't bath him, I couldn't carry him upstairs – I was terrified. I thought, 'If I can't feed him, I might drop him, I might break him, I might accidentally kill him.' It was horrible.

And there was one night I was on this forum, chatting to Heather, and I admitted to her how bad I was feeling, and she stood in and she sorted me out, and I got really friendly with quite a few girls on that site. From then, I kind of realised that everybody needs other people. They don't necessarily have to be people from next door that you can get cups of tea from – they can be someone on a forum, someone on Facebook, someone on Twitter, anyone who can reach out to you.

I've always known that I've had mental health issues. And I was frightened of getting close to people because I didn't want to be a burden. I felt I was weak and I was needy and I needed pity and all those kinds of things, which I know is ridiculous now. I can remember being terrified, absolutely terrified, of them turning round and saying, 'No, I don't want to be your friend.' But I have such a lovely network of people, and I love the bones of them. I just adore them – they've been with me through so much. And, hopefully, I've been there for them and we've all kind of stuck together. And I don't think any of us have met, and I think that's incredibly powerful.

It's lovely that you can have such a strength of feeling towards somebody you haven't actually met.

24. He Was Dancing to Right Said Fred

I am feeling cheeky and light-headed! Last night I slept high up in the hills, amongst the clouds that streamed across Loch Awe, with just the sky and the sheep for company: a would-be-shepherd shivering in the cooling breeze. Now I am back to earth and hungry. There you are, smiling, shy. The local store is safe in your hands.

•

We met when he was dancing to Right Said Fred, 'I'm Too Sexy', and he decided to take his top off when he was dancing! How many years have we been together now? About twenty-four years, and we've had two children. But it doesn't feel like twenty-four years – oh my God no! I know everything about him. I know what he's going to say before he says it. It's good because I know what he's going to do before he does it, because he's very cheeky. He's good fun.

He's such a good dad. I wouldn't say he's a better dad than I am a mum but he's so good, he's so patient – oh he's great. I knew he would always be a good dad because he was such a nice person. My daughter is twenty-one and my son is seventeen. My daughter will phone him every night needing advice for this, for that – oh aye, aha. She lives down in a very remote, very beautiful place. She's a farmer. She was born very premature – she was born eleven weeks early. And he was so good. He held her before I could, and she was literally tiny, but he was straight in there. It was a Caesarean, so he went with her in the lift up to intensive care 'cause I didn't know what had happened.

I love children. I'm desperate for grandchildren – I'm desperate for that next chapter. I'd love to have had more but my two were both in special care for weeks and weeks and weeks. I couldn't go through that again.

25. A Cake on the Doorstep

Family. The ties of blood and connection cord us together strongly though we have barely met. The following day you walk out with me into a torrential deluge. Each droplet of rain bounces hard off the tarmac – my eyes are waterlogged. You walk straight into the downpour, feet pumping, arms pounding, heart bristling. But you soften, too, as the miles go by, and share a little of your journey.

•

I work in the hospice to give something back to them because they looked after my sister. My sister died at 7.20 p.m. The night-shift hospice lady who looked after my sister at home had had a long shift – she was there from 10 a.m. to 7.30 p.m. and she went home and baked a cake and came back and put it on the doorstep. So it's in memory of her baking a cake after a really long and hard shift. She'd been with my sister about a week, so she got very close to her.

I do hairdressing. Drive them up the wall, I do! I started off in reception, and then they were short in the hairdressing so I said I would go in and do the afternoons until they found someone, and I've been there ever since. It's great fun! It's a thank-you for the cake on the doorstep, which I thought was a lovely thing to do. And I've often wondered how she got on and what she's doing now.

They give a lot back to you as well, I must say. You get an awful lot back. You get a lot of happiness from helping other people, particularly at the hospice. The lady whose funeral was today – she gave me so many cuddles when my mother was driving me up the wall. This woman hadn't had a day of illness in her life and then, all of a sudden, she's faced with death. But she took time to make sure I was alright at times. Life is so important – yes, that's it, life is so important. And you realise it yourself as well when you're in a situation like that and someone gives you a cuddle because your mum's been on the phone twenty times a day. When they give you a cuddle it's nicer than the neighbour over the road who says, 'Oh dear, I'm sorry about that.'

It's more meaningful because they understand the meaning of life – because they have a limited life.

26. That's the Deal

You arrive, an energetic bundle of movement and presence. Comfortably sitting in the chair opposite, willing, open and generous. I feel strangely drawn back to my childhood, listening to adults tell tales and stories, quietly attentive in some hidden corner.

.

I was a year at Hilfield Friary, testing my vocation as a Franciscan novice, and I asked my Guardian if I could see a bit of action because I always wanted to do the inner city thing! I was already a priest, which was a little bit unusual. They decided to dispatch me to the East End of Glasgow, where I would live on a 'big scheme' and I'd help out with what they'd call the East End churches – the Episcopal churches in the East End of Glasgow. So we were next to 'Paradise' (Celtic Park), one of the most socio-economically deprived areas in the whole of the UK. Well, I just fell in the love with the whole experience, the people and everything else. You're dealing with that grinding poverty, that lack of hope, serious unemployment. When I was ordained, I thought, 'This is how I'm going to spend my life.'

Probably the most powerful witness to love in Barrowfield – what people appreciated the most – was that we volunteered to be there. It's pretty violent. They called it 'the rule of the baseball bat', and that wasn't far off. Certainly, for my own part, and I'm sure for my fellow brothers, you wanted to identify with those people in some way. I remember working in the East End of London and reading David Sheppard's book *Bias to the Poor*. I remember reading that and thinking, 'That's it. That's the deal. That's what you go and do.' This is doctrine of the incarnation; you are just there. The fact that you've chosen to be there, that's where you wanted to be. In my case, where I requested to be. That was the supreme act of love.

So while in Barrowfield I spent each Sunday going off to help in three other small communities. And by far the largest was St John's, Baillieston, on the outer eastern suburb of Glasgow. It was my first sung Eucharist at St John's. We placed the gospel book on the altar. I went to the altar to pick up the gospel book, burled round and made my way down the aisle. In the far corner I could clearly see this woman standing there. And I thought, 'Goodness, gracious me. Why is there such an attractive, well-dressed women in this church?' Let's just say she absolutely stood out! Now this isn't very Franciscan, but I'm very into cars. I just said rather loudly, in the back of the church as people were filing out, 'Whose is the red Beamer in the car park?' Needless to say, this same woman goes into her pocket, takes her car keys out and gives them a wave! And I thought, 'Well, that fits!' Of course, because of the nature of my work there, this woman and I were meeting on quite a regular basis, and basically a relationship developed during my time in Barrowfield, and I wasn't there all that long, only a matter of months, actually. I knew I had to leave because my allotted time working alongside the Franciscans in Barrowfield had come to an end. After that, I had to go into a period of 'Enclosure' which is, you shuffle off, in this case to the middle of a field in central Worcestershire for seven months, and I wasn't allowed out. And I was hardly allowed to speak. But we could write. We wrote very long letters to each other.

At the end of my time in Enclosure I was instructed to go on retreat for a while. And I went to Whitby and I read a book by Scott Peck called *The Road Less Travelled*. And I didn't even get to the end of the book. I was probably about two-thirds of the way through it and I thought, 'Before I commit myself to the Franciscans, I need to test whether this woman and I should be together.' And that was a very tough decision because I spent years thinking I would be a Franciscan. But I'd met this person who I'd fallen in love with and I thought, 'We need to see whether this is for real or not.' My family had a long association with the Franciscans, so the fact that I was a priest and I was joining the Franciscans, that wasn't all that outrageous. Leaving and then saying, 'I've found this woman who I'm contemplating marrying' – that was considered seriously radical, that was counter-cultural! So there was all of that to deal with. And it was not just brave on my part, but very much for her as well.

I went back to my Novice Guardian and I said, 'Look, I need to go back to Glasgow and look at this seriously before I continue my Franciscan vocation.' And he said, 'Then that's what you have to do.' So I was released – they let me go very graciously – and I went up to Glasgow to spend time with her. We then decided we wanted to be alongside each other.

I'm very much an intuitive animal. I come from the gut. My

mother was a professional theologian and she operated in the head, although she had a big heart. I'm very much in the gut. I've done a lot of zazen in my time, and it's the pit of your stomach, just above your groin, that's the core of your being. And that's where I'm coming from, so I just follow that.

It's been an extraordinary journey. We often reflect on the call to step out of the boat, to take the risk, and it was a big jump for both of us. But we'll be marking our twentieth wedding anniversary on the 19th of May this year. And I would say it's just been a glorious journey. I'd like to think I lived out what I teach and preach. I'd go to the stake for her. And that goes on. It doesn't diminish. We say to each other that we love each other more maybe than when we started. I think that's probably true.

It is that coming together of two human beings, and, for us, we both have an intense spirituality. At that level, it's extraordinary, really – it is genuinely the journey of two souls merging and connecting with the divine.

27. I'm Worth Loving

All day long, your words stay with me. I carry them in my pockets, along with stones and feathers and crumbs. They balance with the rock, the endless path, the rivulets and streams, the rising hills. I am moving through sacred land, alignments marking the way. The earth feels immovable and certain.

•

I struggled. I didn't feel for a long time that I was worthy of loving myself. And it's not that long ago that I came to the realisation that, yeah, I'm worth loving. And I had meditation one morning before I'd gone out to work, and it just kind of hit me. I was guided in this meditation that I had to tell my counsellor, I had to say to her, 'I love me.' And I went all around the houses. But then I said to myself, 'I'm going to go for it – I'm going to say it.' And then the words came. And it was like, it was like a big load had been lifted from me. I used to think that I had to see to everyone else around and about me and see that they were OK, and then, if there was any time left, give it to myself. But I've come to understand that if I look after me I'm a better person for everyone round and about me. And I've had to learn to put me first, which was very, very hard because I'd never done it my whole life – well, my adult life! I think when you're a mum, you put your kids first, then, when you're a gran, you put your grandkids first.

Everyone else is more important than you.

28. Are We Just Worm Food?

En route to Barra, across the Sea of the Hebrides, the currents churn the stomach. I lie on my back, keeping it all inside! An internal tumult and an external clatter of children climbing, crawling, lying. And your story is rising and falling with the current. The minutes drift by. Ahead, the Isles I've longed to see all my life appear as an apparition of whales surfing on the water's horizon.

•

I was very much searching for something – some kind of meaning to life, some purpose. I'd achieved all my material desires, reaching my career ambitions after graduating university. I had the job, and the view from the ivory tower looked like a bit of a wasteland. So I took a gap year at that point and went up to the Black Isle for a year. I was thinking I would travel the world and find myself, but I ended up in the Black Isle, going on an interior journey to discover myself.

So I was twenty-four, wondering what life was all about. Are we just worm food? So I was having a few suicidal thoughts and tendencies. I woke up one night and the world just didn't make sense to me any more. I just felt like my mind was dissolving away. Everything I thought life was supposed to be just didn't make sense.

Then, something. I don't know how you would describe it – a trans-internal vision, a near-death experience, a hallucination. But to me, the outcome in the morning was that there was a God that loved me very much and forgave me for all my transgressions and just wanted me to be a better person. At that point I went back to church – the next morning. I felt this internal prompting to 'Go to church, go to church, go bare foot.' And I thought, 'My goodness, they'll think I'm nuts. They'll arrest me.' And I thought, 'You know what? I'll go like Jesus – I'll wear sandals!' That was my compromise!

So I went back to church and went there for a couple of months or so, but I very much didn't feel nourished and I ended up in the New Age for the next five years or so, seeking 'something'. And I remember looking at the different traditions – looking at the Hindu, the Vedantic traditions and writings and so on. I found the Upanishads were somewhat like the parables in the Christian Bible. I really found this sweetness and nourishment in them. And then I looked at some Sufi stuff as well and that kind of poetic romanticism, and I was thinking, 'Wow, I wish I could find this in my own backyard, in Christianity.' So I tried to go back to the church at that time as well, but it didn't work out.

I was over in Broxburn and I met this visiting little Irish priest and he introduced me to a lady who I got chatting with, and we met over a period of six months. I had some pretty fundamental struggles with my faith and we talked through some of them.

She gave me some prophetic writings from a woman from the Greek Orthodox tradition who'd been receiving divine revelation for the last twenty years. So I started reading them and very much began to find this nourishment that I'd seen in other traditions. I was maybe a few months into reading these. I was grappling. I felt as though this almighty battle was going on inside me of 'Do I accept this? Do I not?' And then I gave my intellectual assent that yes, I believed.

So, at that point, I would have been coming up to thirty. My friend, who introduced me to these writings, said, 'There's somebody over in Germany who's opening her house for the World Youth Day of Prayer. Do you want to go?' I thought, 'That's for those uber-Christians – no thanks!' But I was also thinking, 'Hey, I'm thirty and it's for thirty-year-olds – I'd better go if I'm gonna go!' So I got there and these crazy Christians were getting up at seven in the morning to go and pray and stuff, and I thought, 'Oh, you're kidding!' So I went downstairs to where they had this wee chapel and thought, 'I'll get a wee seat at the back.' So, I'm sitting down at the back and two young women start singing at the front, and it literally sounds like voices of angels. And I thought, 'Wow, wow, who is that?' So I met Jana, one of these 'angels'. She didn't have much English, and the little English she did have didn't translate well into a thick Scottish accent!

So the following year, there was another ecumenical pilgrimage in Turkey and Greece. We were maybe five hundred people from seventeen different churches, in twelve different buses – and she was sitting in front of me! So, for about a week, I'd tried to grab these sideways glances. I was like, 'Ah no, she saw me, she saw me!' But I had a 'coach', the guy I was sharing my room with. He was giving me some advice and he'd said to me, 'You should spend the day with her – you should ask her to spend the day with you tomorrow.' So we were going on the ferry over to Patmos the next day, and on the ferry I asked, 'Is it OK if we spend the day together?' She said, 'Yeah, that's fine.' We had the day together and had many laughs and conversations. In the evening there was a couple that were getting married in the Orthodox church. The bride had been on our bus and asked everyone to come along for the wedding feast. So we went along and we had dinner. There wasn't much dancing, or not that we were doing anyway. It was getting to the end of the evening and time to go home, so I said, 'Ah, will I take you home?' And she said, 'Yeah, that will be nice.'

So we started walking along to the hotel and didn't want the evening to end. 'Shall we go for a walk along the beach?'

'Yeah, let's walk along the beach.' So we get to the end of the beach and it's like, 'Shall we walk back?'

'Yeah, let's do that.'

'Oh, shall we walk back again?'

'Yeah, let's walk back again!'

And I'm getting a wee bit fed up with walking all this time so I say, 'Shall we sit down?' So we found a wee rock that we could sit down on at least and we're chatting away. Having suffered a few rejections in my time, I thought, 'You know what? We'll edge our way in slowly here. I'll test the water!' I asked, 'What would you rather? Would you rather I came to Prague to see you again for a date, or would you rather we got engaged?' So what I heard was 'Oh yes, that would be lovely.' At this point, Jana understands that we were getting engaged. I was thinking, 'OK, that's a good answer. That sounds good she'd want to get engaged!'

So then I plucked up the courage and asked, 'Would you marry me?'

And she said, 'Yes, of course, as soon as possible.'

A few hours before that we were on the bus from the church to the reception and I was sitting down and I was thinking, 'You know what? If she takes my hand, I know we're getting married.' But it was very much I wasn't just giving her my hand, I was giving her my heart. I wasn't holding anything back. And she took my hand and I thought, 'OK, that's it.'

So from two years and not quite managing it to five months after our first date, we were married. Nine years and four children later, this is us! When you come into that place of knowing, where you just know that something is right, something is for you, there is no opposite, there is no 'other' – you are just in 'flow'. It was like levitating, like you're scraping yourself off the stars, off the ceiling. But it was very internal. You just knew it in the depth of your being. In your core. This is it. This is right.

29. To Be Part of Something

The ferry arrives. I try to picture you in my mind. Until now you have been a complex thread of Twitter feeds, of emails and images. I make my way from the ferry to the shop, staff in hand, and there you are, as promised. Hours later, I am sitting comfortably in your front room. The setting sun reflects its light on the gentle swell of the sea in the bay. I am finally here, the Hebrides – 'home'.

•

We decided, wouldn't it be good if we could get people to send us bunting, like a flag? And wouldn't it be nice if it involved people from all over the world? And it's nice for people to be able to be part of something and leave something behind. Make a project out of it, make it mean something! And it's also part of social history as well. Why people feel connected to the place. So we send a little archive sheet with your bunting about what your connection is with the island. And through that we get some amazing stories of why people have come here, or perhaps they've lived here all their life. And some people, you know, they put a lot of thought into it. We had this family last year who came from the States. They all did one, and they all put a lot into it – bits of themselves. It was amazing how much they'd thought about their bunting, and they were really leaving a part of themselves here.

I suppose I will always feel like an outsider, a little bit. You're not of the place. I've chosen to be here. You know, I couldn't take my husband away from this – it's his home. He's a fisherman. Where else would we live? We couldn't have this standard of living anywhere else – we've got a nice house and we've got a bit of land, and that gives you a certain freedom. You can do things – we can have bees, we can have hens. So we can survive because we've got a bit of land. If we were to move to somewhere else we wouldn't have that, we wouldn't be able to afford that. Plus the kids love it. They're so much freer; they get a proper childhood. You don't have to worry for them so much.

I didn't know anybody when I came here. I came for a job. I worked in Citizens Advice. It was on the first of December. The weather was awful. The boat was delayed, and there were two of us on the boat for an interview and it would only wait for one of us to have the interview, so one of us would have to stay. The other woman had family – she was dead worried about getting back. I was just temping at the time because I'd been travelling, so I said, 'Well, you go back – I'll just stay.' They told me while I was here, because I had to stay the whole weekend, that I had the job, so that gave me the chance to look for accommodation.

So I was staying in a B&B and I was eating in a pub and this older man, Roddy, came up to me and said, 'Oh, you don't want to be having your dinner here. Come back to my house for sup.' And I looked at the barmaid and she went, 'Ach, off you go, you'll be fine.' So I ate at his house – he's very hospitable. During this time, I met his nephew, Wallace – my future husband. After I'd eaten, he took me back to the B&B and then drove me around a bit for the rest of the weekend.

When I came back to the island to live, Uncle Roddy had gone back to sea so Wallace was the only person I recognised. However, it took him nine months to speak to me sober! He was so shy. I used to walk as I didn't have a car. I lived in Skallary and walked to Castlebay every day. One day he stopped the car, coming back from fishing, and he said, 'I'm going to the pub tonight if you fancy coming along.' And somebody had told me that he might have feelings for me. The conversation had got round about this new girl on the island and what a nutter she was for doing all the walking – and he kind of stuck up for me a bit.

So I came for a job and I ended up getting married!

30. Don't I Know You from Somewhere?

You find time this morning to take me out, along the coast, back to where my walk had finished the previous day. We are searching for a whale washed up on the shore. Standing there in coats, with the wind swirling and blowing rain in our faces, I feel a sense of completeness. You leave and I gaze out on the Atlantic, wondering if another soul looks back at me.

•

N: We actually lived in the same cul-de-sac. I was a student nurse and Bill was a strange-looking guy with long hair and faded jeans but carrying a briefcase. And the girls I shared a flat with, the student nurses, thought, 'I wonder what he does.' When we began as student nurses, we had to live in the nurses' home and then, at the end of the first year, they suddenly changed the rules and we all scarpered and got houses – and we all ended up in this little cul-de-sac.

B: I thought that Norma, she was really snooty, she wouldn't have anything to do with me.

N: Not quite the case. One of the girls in the house fancied Bill and I thought, 'I'm not getting involved there!' I probably *was* snooty as well! We went our separate ways. Bill left first – he had set out on an overland trip and ended up in Australia. Three years later I was in a pub heading to a party when Bill walked in and, at first, he didn't recognise me.

B: I was teaching in Manchester, having just returned from Australia, and a friend of mine – one of the guys in the department – said he was having a party. And I was invited to meet in this pub before the party on a Saturday night. And so I went round to this pub and met Roger and his gang. I can't quite remember what it was – there was something about the assembled group that was going to this party, but I thought, 'I'm not particularly keen!' So I made my apologies and said I didn't feel like a party. And so I looked around after they'd gone and I saw a guy at the bar who had been a friend of the guy I had been to Australia with. And I looked at him for a while and I thought, 'It is, it's Eric! I'll go over and have a word.' So I go across and say, 'Hello,' and I actually realise that he's talking to a lady next to him. And this was Norma. And I looked at her and said, 'Don't I know you from somewhere?'

N: So he tells me all about his trip to Australia, 'cause I know he's been to Australia, and he goes on and on and on and on! And I'm actually chocolate brown at this stage but he assumes I haven't left Manchester! Eventually he gets round to saying, 'What have you been doing?' 'I just spent two years up the Amazon, as a midwife and trained nurse.'

B: I thought she was joking! Hey, she looked absolutely stunning. She had her South American dress on and she was as brown as a berry. We went on to a party. Having just said, 'No, I don't fancy a party,' Norma said, 'I'm just on the way to a party', so I said, 'Ooh, yes, I'll come!'

I always look back and think it wasn't a place I ever went to – it wasn't a part of Manchester I frequented.

N: I'd never been in that pub before.

B: So that was the really curious thing about it. This chance meeting!

N: A year later we got married.

B: When I suggested to Norma that we might get married, we were down some lane somewhere.

N: Really?

B: Don't you remember that? I can't remember which bit, of which particular lane, or where it was, but we were in the countryside!

N: For me, that summer, I worked in a social work department in Moss Side. Everyone was getting married, and I thought, 'I can't be doing with this – I don't like all this dressing up!' We had a civil wedding, a Registry Office wedding, which suited us fine. It was like a day out and we went back to work, didn't we? Our honeymoon was a day in the Peak District!

I think it's comfortable and it's friendship and it's security and it's part of who we are. We argue and bicker, but a lot of people see us as being independent – we both do a lot of things independently but we have a solid relationship from which to do that, and it works for us. We don't conform to what many couples here will see as a marriage. You know, we don't have kids and I will just take off and go and do my own stuff and go away. And then the other thing is that when I have a lot of girlfriends that come in, Bill will just say, 'Who wants a cup of tea?' and they'll all say, 'My husband would never do that!' So we both break the mould for here.

I kind of assume that Bill will always go first because he's five and a half years older than me. That's not to say he will, but I don't know if I would stay here. I mean the other issue that comes up is decrepitude and dementia. I'm healthy and robust and enjoying life, but none of us knows what's around the corner! How we would want to be cared for and/or not – you know, to end life if life got too much physically, emotionally, pain-wise, whatever! And how you handle that.

B: R.D. Laing said, I can't quote it but it was basically, 'The worst possible thing that can happen to you is that you can lose the person you are most fond of.' That is it – 'the most traumatic thing that you experience'.

31. We're Definitely Coming Home

Inquisitive. Open. Here the river cuts its way through to the sea, on the west coast of Uist. Tobha Mor, sacred land. Sheltering from the burning wind, safely held in communion with this couple and their children. Seeking home, seeking time. Above, the clouds move by endlessly as the day draws in.

•

A: You hear all this stuff about people – especially 'men don't communicate', very stoical and all that. I find that people don't really hold that many secrets, you know? People say what they're up to, what they're doing and all that kind of stuff.

Maybe there's a lack of emotional content. They don't put a spin or an opinion into it – but I can't shut people up once they've had a pint, you know. It's also a bit of everyone knows your business anyway, so you might as well broadcast it because people will find out, you know. There are probably about three sets of binoculars pointed at us right now going,

'What the hell are they up to? Who is it anyway? Is that the boy from Minngearraidh?'

We're definitely coming home. How long we'll last is the problem. I think we'll last as a family, as a couple?! I've always wanted to come home and try staying. I'm from South Uist, from just up the road here in Minngearraidh. I keep coming back, and the pull is much greater when you have kids. We come up here and we holiday just about every chance we get. We do travel – we stay in Glasgow and we travel to various different cities and places – but we tend to drift back here all the time, you know. You do know where you're from – I find that. I've always been very strongly from here, even more so than being Scottish or British or whatever, you know.

C: I think the sad thing – why we may not last here – is that Alexander will be commuting from Glasgow for work. That just puts a strain on us, we're not all together kind of thing. But that's the nature of the beast, because there are not that many job opportunities up here. We kind of yearn to be up here. Although I'm from a city, I come from the outskirts, where you're more connected to the natural environment, Dublin being on the coast. Where I grew up there was more green space and the sea and everything like that. So I miss that. But I think, being in Glasgow, there's too much busyness and too much choice. You feel a bit like a battery hen, whereas here you feel like you can breathe a little bit more. And there's more freedom for the kids where they can just have a childhood.

A: I met Christina at my brother's wedding in Ireland. I've got two brothers married in Ireland, and she was there at the second wedding. One thing led to another and here we are, four kids later. I think it was really the Funky Chicken on the dance floor that clinched it. Dressed in kilt, barely aware of my own embarrassment. In fact, not really caring about my own embarrassment. Christina was pals with Susan, my brother's wife, and she came along for the evening bit. She tried to take advantage of me because I was drunk.

C: I actually had doubts that I would make the wedding.

A: I'm sure you regret it every day, but I'm glad you did. That was over seventeen years ago.

C: Seventeen years since I met Alexander. I think it becomes deeper because you go through so many life experiences, and some of them are really hard. And you kind of stick through them and you kind of get to the other side, so it makes the bond much stronger.

A: I think so.

C: There is all of the first meeting, the flush of excitement, and everything is new and stuff like that. There is a bit of that, but it just becomes a bit richer and a bit deeper.

A: It does that, but it becomes busier too and you have less time for stuff, especially when the kiddies come along.

C: You kind of miss each other in the fog of busyness too, yes.

A: I feel like it's not the same seventeen years on. In some ways it's better, in some ways there's a lack of time. I do still love Christina loads and I do think it's harder work to keep that going but, like she said, there's a lot of water under the bridge, a lot of things you go through to get to this stage. I couldn't give it up – I couldn't give up on it. Do you know what I mean? I don't understand, sometimes, when people give up, either at the first sign of difficulty or when they've been through difficulty. Because I think it just keeps on coming round in cycles. We might not have much time for each other just now, but I do think that in the future we'll have more time to spend together and, you know, it's good just now, it's good.

32. Being of Service

Miniature clay boats built to commemorate, shelves of brightly coloured ornaments, hand-crafted objects of every kind, all made and thought-full. A place to sleep below the books, amidst the making. Quiet. Just the wind tapping at the window and the sea's low chorus for company in the darkness.

•

Anything you do of real heart is of service, isn't it? I'm an artist, so my path is making things.

I landed up living in the Western Isles and I've become obsessed with boats, very beautiful boats built by a family on Grimsay. Five generations of a family built these beautiful wooden fishing boats. And I went down to the harbour in Lochmaddy and I saw this beautiful boat and I started drawing it. And then I asked people about it and it turned out it was one of these beautiful boats that had been built on Grimsay. I've been making very, very simplified models of these boats for an exhibition. I think I always wanted to make a lot of them. And this thing about 'the soul journey' has been in the background as well – vessels for lost souls. Here's one! You see, they're very, very simple but rather lovely.

And then I got interested in this whole idea of 'home' and people not having a home and having to journey. And of course, you know the whole history of migration here – people having to leave. And then the whole tragedy in the Mediterranean at the moment and the way that people are drowning. There's something very poignant about these boats, these vessels. I don't think I have answers, but I feel I am called on to serve in some way. But because I don't really know what it is I am doing and I can't speak for it very easily, then it is quite hard to say what that 'service' is. But I want to be of service and I feel, on some level, that's what I'm being called upon to do. You know, what I'm hoping is that I find some sort of interactive aspect to the exhibition that means people can commemorate their own dead or people they feel are lost.

I think it is a privilege to follow your own heart, your own path. It's like you've got a role – a role that people don't really understand but they sort of accept – that allows you to be a bit eccentric, a bit different. To dress differently and behave differently. There's also a lot of fear in it as well, and I think that's what I struggle with – and a lot of creative people struggle with. And it's the fear of the unknown and it's the fear of the internal criticism that goes on, that you lay yourself open to, by attempting to do things other than the dishes! If you see what I mean!

I won't pretend to make great things but I do make heartfelt things, I think. In the process of actually making things it can feel like it's not there, sometimes. I mean, it's not like you feel all the time that you're in this heartfelt connection within. I think the aim for me is to feel that something is coming through me. I think that's part of being of service as well – that something that needs to be expressed comes through me.

33. My Place To Be

Lying back in the grass I feel the wild North Atlantic spread out before me. Not a soul interrupts this perfect vision. The showers come and go and I remain sheltered here, embraced and embracing, consumed by the air and the waves and the light.

·

A lot of young people, when they reach seventeen and eighteen, put their heads down and go to Glasgow and become part of that scene. But almost all of them still look to the islands as home. And people may be away for sixteen or seventeen years or even thirty years, but the islands are still their home.

It's a cord that people feel they are attached to. I came back from Glasgow to stay here because I felt it was my home. There's something about the sea and the sky and the place itself that is in you. And you belong. You have a sense of belonging to something. And being part of something. I come down here and walk on the beach with my dog, and I'm usually the only one here. We never see anyone down here, but this place is where I am — my place to be.

34. I Didn't Believe in Love

The final steps trodden – Callanish. For the briefest moment, I pause to feel that sense of place – to breathe, to commune. Crowds of tourists descend and the shutters of countless cameras whir. I take shelter. Then finally the body relaxes and then lets go. Its work is done for now. Thoughts turn to tea and cake and the removal of boots and socks. A bath perhaps. Stillness. And then just you and me, my love. That pipe, half an ounce of old wood carried five hundred miles – my grandfather's, my father's, my own. To the lowing of ruminants we ruminate, the air rich in toxins and prayer. We sigh out the day and welcome the night, and remember one more story, folded into its deepness.

•

I didn't believe in love. I was very driven – a career woman – and I'd been let down so many times in the past. I was completely cynical about it. I didn't believe that it would ever come through for me. I didn't believe that it would ever mean more to me than myself and earning money and fame and fortune. But the truth of the fact is that I met him and now that's all that there is. And it's all I can see and it's all that I feel, and it's the rest of the world that doesn't make sense now. The most difficult, the most powerful thing I have ever had to do is learn how to love. It's a continual reflection of who you are, how you're behaving and what your thoughts are. And what sort of human being you are is continually reflected back at you by the other person being a mirror to your actions.

So it's been a completely catastrophic and tortuous breakdown of the image of the self that I thought I was. And as you go through those layers, of who it is you think you are and who it is other people think you are, you finally start to come close to the essence of yourself. And when you connect with that other person's essence, when you find it is the essence of your beings that is connected, you realise the essence of your beings is connected to the essence of all the other beings around you – animals, trees, water, the sky. And you're not alone any more and you feel whole somehow. And life, although it is a lot harder to manage, isn't as hard any more because you realise there is something beyond yourself.

Epilogue

Journey's end. After five hundred miles along the path, I find myself looking out over the fields to the stones of Callanish, in the north of the Isle of Lewis. Outside, the snow flurries and the wind blows horizontally – all is alive and in movement. A pair of golden eagles takes refuge in a copse of squat trees. We sit together in silence.

Going on a journey, walking out of your front door and leaving behind those things that cradle you and keep you safe, is not easy for me. I find these journeys hard. I worry. The uncertainty, the letting go, the loosening of constraints challenge my courage – they set me adrift somehow. But in the moment of each departure I feel I gain the chance to experience something essential – the essence of my being. In leaving behind those burdens and layers of protection, I am free to commune with the earth, with myself, with others, with the cosmos. And so I fall into love, into a loving action, walking into a sense of the sacred. Through this motion I experience an uncovering and re-discovering – a journey towards a deeper love and understanding of who I am.

We all journey in our different ways. And though we have destinations and goals, and markers along the way, it is the journey itself that is important. How we move through our life, the connections we make, the intentions we set, the love we offer ourselves, others and this beautiful world, is our greatest potential gift. Because, in the end, 'it doesn't matter what path you walk, what matters is the heart you walk it in'.

Go well
and in love.